Une
Pres

WAVE BOOKS

TISA BRYANT

Afterword by Margo Jefferson

Published by Wave Books

www.wavepoetry.com

Copyright © 2007 and 2024 by Tisa Bryant

Afterword copyright © 2024 by Margo Jefferson

First Wave Books edition 2024

All rights reserved

Wave Books titles are distributed to the trade by

Consortium Book Sales and Distribution

Phone: 800-283-3572 / SAN 631-760X

Library of Congress Cataloging-in-Publication Data

Names: Bryant, Tisa, author.

Title: Unexplained presence / Tisa Bryant.

Description: [Seattle] : Wave Books, 2024.

Includes bibliographical references.

Identifiers: LCCN 2024008733

ISBN 9798891060050 (paperback)

Classification: LCN PN56.3.B55 B79 2024

DDC 809/.89–dc23/eng/20240304

LC record available at https://lccn.loc.gov/2024008733

Unexplained Presence was originally published in 2007 by Leon Works

Designed by Crisis

Printed in the United States of America

9 8 7 6 5 4 3 2 1

IN MEMORY OF MY MOTHER,

FOR EVERY LITTLE THING

Scene Se

election

Black figures in Eurocentric literature, film, and visual art are rarely presented without being given a distinct, racialized function, the import of which often goes largely undisputed, if not wholly unacknowledged, simply because the power of saying, of naming and describing it, has been withheld. The explanation for their presence and their function is hidden in plain sight, a double-sided sleight of hand between the maker and the subconscious, and between the maker and the receiver of the work. This sleight of hand intrigues me. Like watching two people (lovers? spies?) silently mouthing words to each other from across a crowded room, my comprehension of the message occurs surreptitiously. I know things I'm not supposed to know. I see without seeing, and witness an open secret, in a roomful of people where I am not the only one with such eyes.

But, as with lovers and spies and secret codes, we're conditioned not to look too long or too closely at how or why these figures do what they do, how they might perpetuate or debunk myths around race, sexuality, and storytelling. We simply minimize, as needed, their effect on the environment (narrative), and on us, by shielding them, hand to eye, from our view.

The writings in this collection reflect the shifting landscape of racialized narratives, and interrogate this silent contract between maker and reader/viewer. My touchstone here is Toni Morrison's *Playing in the Dark: Whiteness and the Literary Imagination*. Her project is "an investigation into the ways in which a non-white, africanlike (or Africanist) presence or persona was constructed in the United States, and the imaginative uses this fabricated presence served." In this book, I instead explore constructions of black presences in European literature, visual art, and film, simply to underscore the narrative continuum of such presences on either side of the Atlantic, and indeed elsewhere, between painter, author, and auteur.

I consider cinematic language, genre, myth-making, and the authority of the text in recombinant fashion, so as to write the story of a painting or a film while questioning its materiality, while imagining the voice and thought of unexplained presences, turning objects into subjects, metaphorical shorthand into a style of explication. "Old school" black literary criticism meets fictional device and together enters a Virginia Woolf novel or Italian cinema or Surrealist prose. So as to write film, write painting, write what it means to see. (Re)writing and reframing across genre creates a way of "talking the seen," and a form for catching racialized narration in the act of making itself (un)known.

In homage to Roland Barthes, I opted not to reproduce any images in this book, but to instead enter into the foxy realm of myths that images, signs, and metaphors create, and to bring you with me.

Though only one piece in this collection, "Under Cover of Darkness," has been previously published, in 1913: *A Journal of Forms*, several pieces have been aired out over the years. I would like to thank Anne Waldman at Naropa University, Sommer Browning at Pete's Candy Store, Stacy Szymaszek at the Poetry Project at St. Mark's Church, Anna Joy Springer and Naima Lowe at TMI: Too Much Information, Sara Seinberg at K'vetsch, Christopher Stackhouse at Redhead Gallery, Emily Abendroth at Moles not Molars, and the Warwick Museum of Art for the opportunity to share and understand the sound of this work. Many thanks to Rhode Island School of Design's Part-Time Faculty Development Fund for its generous financial support.

Unexplained Presence is the result of countless conversations, and has benefited from the support, care, friendship, love, criticism, and laughter I've shared with so many people. My love to my family: my father, Donald, my brother, Howard, my sister, Taryn, and all the Bryants, Downes, Paiges, Tylers and Browns. Deep gratitude to Renee Gladman, Andre Thompson, Ana-Maurine Lara, and Esther Figueroa for their encouragement, patience and repeated readings of each iteration of this book, to Wura-Natasha Ogunji for taking every word into her hands, to Jeff Clark for his intuitive design in collaboration with the text, and to Jaime Cortez, R. Erica Doyle, and John R. Keene for their invaluable responses to the book that emerged. My devotion to The Village and the Encyclopedists. Very special thanks to Angela Y. Davis, Nancy Armstrong, Dorothy Denniston, Brian Evenson, Diana George, Arlene Keizer, Thalia Field, the Dark Room Collective, Carole Maso, and Laylah Ali: your words continue to echo. And finally, again and always, my undying love to the spirit of my mother, Nona Lesley Downes Bryant.

UNEXPLAINED PRESENCE

ILLUSTRATION
S.H. GRIMM, *Drolleries*
JUNE 14, 1771
PRINT COLLECTION,
LEWIS WALPOLE LIBRARY
YALE UNIVERSITY

An old woman in a humble cloak stops, thunderstruck, at the sight of a euphemistic "lady of fashion," emerging from an avenue of lindens.

Behind her trails a black page in ornate suiting, a plumed turban on his head, her lapdog tucked in his arms. He, too, is the mark of fashion among such of the period, who promoted their charms within sight of the well-heeled.

The lady's hair is teased to an exaggerated height that rises into the trees. At the summit of her coiffure sits a ribboned hat. The old woman must lean back and scope with her hand cupped around her eye in order to take it all in. Her wrinkled hand reaches for her heart in dismay. Her mouth drops open.

"Heyday!" reads the caption. "Is this my daughter Anne?"

DARLING

We begin with a white frame, a billboard of emaciated children from foodless nations, figured in charcoal and stippled inks, glimpsed as if through fast blinking eyes. Knobby legs. Ashen skin. Thin hair and cracked lips. Africa, South Asia, Latin America. The watching body backs away. Blink. There. The scaffold is revealed, along with a white-suited man wielding a brush. Scenes of starvation are quickly papered over with the face of Honeyglow Cosmetics' "Ideal Woman." Blonde, victorious, Diana Scott, smiling, fine-tuned, hair swinging carefree over London's soft-focus bustle. Those lips. Those eyes. Those dark and morbid bones beneath the teeth.

Diana speaks from an unseen present, perhaps still in the seat of celebrity, chattering to someone in the shadows. She tells the tale of how she slept her way to the top modeling jobs with shameless aplomb. Diana is Julie Christie. Everyone loves Julie Christie! Her conniving manipulations, bratty infidelities, are almost innocent. Everyone calls her Darling. She is everyone's darling. Even this film is named for her. And yet there is someone else telling this story, her story that is another story running alongside, keeping up, keeping track. The story of poverty and its underbelly, indifference, trots lockstep with our Darling's opportunism. And she's oblivious, it seems, of her nemesis. Her voice intones flippantly over a mise-en-scène that damns her. Her voice turns people into objects that can still, and quite often do, point the finger. And so John Schlesinger's indictment of "fashion" and celebrity, circa 1965, begins.

Dirk Bogarde squints, interested. "Super." "Ghastly."

Dirk and Darling flirt.

He is married, two children, an attached house in a modest suburb, dark-haired wife once loved, now habitual, left standing in the driveway at the threshold of kitchen and dinette, baby on hip, mouth ajar. He doesn't name his reason for leaving. (Darling!) He moves in with Diana. He writes, interviews philosophers, maintains a serious, aloof manner. His eyes are cold and dark, but he is smitten. She prances about the apartment, looking pretty and bored. He types. She flounces, scribbling flippant messages in white grease pencil on the mirror above the fireplace, tiptoes to the window, kicking her heels up on the couch, smoking, then flits out into the hallway, a sudden noise in her ears. Two black men in suede and velvet pantsuits, expensive leather shoes like twin Puss 'n' Boots, scud up the marble steps. They greet her almost unintelligibly.

"Happy Christmas, baby," their voices slur in unison.

"Happy Christmas!" she calls brightly, leaning riskily over the railing, then whirling back to Dirk.

"Darling," Diana says. "Darling, two of the most *gorgeous*

Negroes you have ever seen have just gone up the stairs. What on earth is going on up there?"

"They're having a diplomatic reception," he says. "Would you like to have a diplomatic reception?"

Would she ever! We don't see them invite the party into their flat. We don't see Diana, our Darling, "receive" anyone "diplomatically." The action is elsewhere. No more close shots of suede crotches or West Indian skins. Diana and Dirk escape into their bedroom, away from the partying multiracial crowd, "gorgeous Negroes," yes, but more than Diana's curiosity can handle. Dirk and Diana huddle together on the floor behind the bed, wanting everyone to leave. This dalliance into diplomacy with Negroes yields nothing of value for Diana's career, and so, as she did her poor husband ten minutes into the film, she drops it flat.

Diana does another ad for Honeyglow. It's everywhere. To promote herself, she agrees to emcee a raffle at an exclusive charity event. The room is bursting with hoi polloi, sequins, black ties, high-rolling hair, and trussed up executives. The event is attended by several young black boys, eight or ten years old, dressed as pages in ornately designed jackets and powdered wigs, totally liveried, proffering trays of dainties.

"I hate doing charity work," our Darling intones.

The black boys bend, offer, are ignored. A charitable executive gives a speech full of exquisite pauses.

"I'm sure I have no need to bring to your ... attention ...

the plight of our ... brothers ... of every ... creed ... race and color ..."

A gilded woman touches up her makeup; another salivates at the charity roulette wheel.

"... in every far-flung corner of the earth ..."

Our eyes are brought to rest on three black pages at the rear of the ballroom, their backs pressed against the wall.

"... who at this ... very moment ..."

Roulette wheel. Sandwiches. What exquisite teeth, Darling! What dark and morbid bones beneath. Pray tell, who preys upon these children? Upon their mothers and fathers? Pray look upon the mark, juxtaposed against such civilization. What gets worked out through this direction, through black children in powdered wigs, who ...

"... are suffering the humiliation, degradation, shame ... of the agonies of malnutrition."

Without applause, we move to a queen in a tux, one Lord Grout. He greets the organizer of the event, and the executive head of our Darling's Honeyglow campaign, Miles. Miles is Laurence Harvey, tall, mod, and smug. Lord Grout has been losing at roulette.

He tells Miles, "I like your black boys. I don't suppose I could wrap one up and take him home?"

"They're all numbered," says Miles. "I wouldn't try to change your luck if I were you."

Lord Grout sniffs, irritated, and walks to the head of the

flying buttress, where one of the pages stands. The Lord pauses, passes, looking leeringly over his shoulder. The boy in his gaze is distant but vulnerable, eyes spotting something unseen that keeps his back rigid, that keeps his head from spinning. Lord Grout sighs and lumbers down the stairs, his prospects for the evening nil.

To increase her prospects, Diana sleeps with Miles, who then takes her to a party.

We segue into a cinema verité truth game. A 16mm projector shoots a white frame of light onto the party wall.

"When the music stops, the cradle will rock," lisps a black man to the crowd, his accent thick, his gestures sweet. This man is South African actor Zakes Mokae. As soon as he moves, "jungle music" begins playing from some unknown source. Syncopation. Congas and flute. The players romp around in a circle, dancing, frolicking, shrieking shadows flung, stripping off and exchanging clothes. Buck wild! There's screaming. Cowbells. Then silence. Mokae fills the frame of light. He wears a frosted blonde wig and a white frilly blouse.

A severe chisel-faced woman calls out, "Why Diana Scott, how you've *changed!*"

"Why Darling," our wigged Mokae purrs. "It's certainly because I've had too much *sundry*." He twirls a frosted lock curled at his cheek, smiling coyly at his pun.

"Ahhh!" cries the party.

"*Combien de fois?*" someone asks.

"I don't understand the français."

"How many times?"

He flutters his eyelashes.

A burly man inquires, "Will you come on a cruise with me to . . ."

Diana's black doppelganger cuts in. "Only if I have the top bed."

"Haaa!" cries the party.

He's doing our Darling well. Miles is bemused, watching. So is another hunk of stuff. "What would you do to be in my next film, Diana?" he asks.

"I don't know, but I'll definitely do it."

"Raaah!" The crowd lets air out in joyous waves. Miles laughs loudly. Our actual Darling, also dressed in white, is perturbed. By now it's easy to forget that *Darling* is narrated by our Darling, looking back at her career. So it's easy not to question why she'd retell *this* episode of her story. Darling never says how she felt. It's not a particularly self-reflexive moment. It's Schlesinger who's on about the manufacturing of white privilege and greed through images of its own beauty and goodness. What makes *this* read of Darling Diana Scott, vis-à-vis a black man's parody of her, more visually necessary, more pertinent than any other? A kind of tough love from not-yo-mama. Whose child is she, anyway?

Heyday, is this my Daughter Anne?

"I don't understand," our Darling pouts to the severe-faced woman. "Is he supposed to be me?"

"Yes," Severe Face tells her.

"But why?"

"Because it's fun," Severe Face replies. And everyone *does* seem to be having a good time. And yet this man, Mokae, jabbing at our Darling's morality and ethics, her unbounded ambition, this black man isn't trying to have a diplomatic reception. There is no diplomacy, but a well-studied caricature from someone who, we think, is a total stranger to Diana. The white frame of light a truth space, a provocation, phosphorescent about the head of a kittenish black queen.

What makes me the Ideal Revelator, Mokae says to us, behind his cupped hand. This Darling is not my concern. I do me better. But who'll watch? All and sundry?

His blond wig bounces. With a giggle our doppelganger's head flips back, the wig flies off, he becomes an unknown presence again, the conga-flute music takes him stepping, primitive, out of the frame. Severe Face returns and stands in the white light. Her thin lips are so cruelly pursed. With a jerk of a bony arm, she thrusts a fetish of black wood into the truth frame. It's dark and mysterious as a coconut, in the shape of a face, hair sprouting from its nose and brow. Severe Face brandishes the mask, as if in statement. Diana is horrified. The crowd goes silent and the flute is cut short as the woman's stern white face disappears behind the grimacing black mask.

Relation is not made up of things that are foreign but of shared knowledge.

EDOUARD GLISSANT "The Open Boat"

SOMETHING IN THE AIR

On the floorplanks at the portside house, a cockroach scrambles underfoot, antennae feeling out the atmosphere of Fanny Price's squalid home. Her mother looks grim, her father drunk. A number of indifferent boy children, and a tiny girl, scamper and pout. Fanny links arms with her sister, full of feeling. This is a different Fanny Price than the one invented by Jane Austen in the novel *Mansfield Park*. This Fanny Price is a bit mouthy, a bit wild, a more *amalgamated* Fanny Price, created for film by Patricia Rozema. A Fanny Price whose very spirit is siphoned from the life of Austen herself. This is cinema. And this Fanny Price is off for an experiment in change and ethical fortitude. But first, she must be a child. What kind of child? A special child, a perceptive child. One who hears a voice few in her future will be willing to explain.

The scene begins.

Off she goes, Tiny Miss Disheveled, looking back aghast at her mother's already turned back, no waving good-bye, no tear wiped on an index finger. The child steps into a waiting carriage. The sea glimmers in the gray heat of a cloud-covered sun. Out there, leagues away, is something. Someone. Who sings? See the copper on the hull? That marks it as a slave ship. See the white birds straining against the rich breeze? They are not doves of peace and love, but scavengers of opportunity. Child Fanny Price is sent to live with rich relations of the absentee planter class. She is being pitched out of poverty, all for the betterment of her mind, and her prospects. So let her first lesson begin here, not yet at the site of prosperity, but on the road winding to it. Jaunty violin strings pitched to the journey give way to an unseen African figure, crying out from afar on the ship with the copper hull in the glimmering gray sea. The wailing grows over the water, reaches toward the child, a voice shaped like a pointing black finger gloved in a white feminist hand.

"Oh no!" cries the crowd.

We lean forward with poor Child Fanny out of the carriage port toward the sound. The driver stops above the ocean on a cliff, tethers the horse to a tree. To lament. Beyond the cliff, on the sea, a single ship three masts high from which a single voice from Mali emanates. In the control room, russet-haired Patricia Rozema reduces the volume of singer Salif Keita's wailing to a whisper. We barely hear it before it's clipped off. Text Fanny Price, a cut-out paper doll covered in fine print, cups one ear and covers the other. Rozema stares hard between the mannered lines that make up Text Fanny's dress.

"Do you hear that?" Child Fanny says to the carriage driver.

Driver nods. "Black cargo, miss."

"Black cargo?" Child Fanny repeats.

"Yes," Driver says. "Probably some ship's doctor or heroic captain brought home a few darkies as gift for the wife."

That's a mouthful, Driver.

Child Fanny's smooth brow wrinkles at the ill-formed idea, a disembodied voice from an enslaved body, produced on the occasion of her ascent into wealth. She'll speak of "it," pointedly but privately, to Edmund, the planter's son, her love, her moral foil. There's something to be said for that.

Fanny keeps to the edges, not quite first class in the household, as her Aunt Norris is quick to remind her. Her girl cousins are indulged and smug. She reads, she writes, she morphs into a third, a fourth body. Fanny Austen. Fanny Austen Rozema. History dull? Invention? Don't disturb this groove. The charm, the romance. It's all in the (un)making! Don't think of how infrequently they bathed. Don't grapple, viewer, with any difficulty with the marriage scheme. That Edmund, the soulmate (and first cousin!) of miss peaches and cream might instigate scenes of subjection elsewhere, even upon his own children from his black mistress. O speak obliquely, if at all, of History and its slaves. Not Our slaves, but History's. It is wild, too wild. The mass cult of Austen wants it tamed. They roar from the jungle of classic books. The cult of England. And the United States. For there is no one alive now who can be held responsible for what happened then. For "it." No one alive now benefits from "its" existence. This is romance. Back to the time when we had it made. Who's, whose, we? Hush now. Don't explain. Rozema, rabble-rouser, raises an eyebrow.

Grown now, Fanny screams like a banshee, chasing down the bendable Edmund with energetic running. Wild Fanny, naturally boisterous, but corrected often by Sir Thomas and the glaring eyes of Aunt Norris. A remembrance of poverty past. Untamed specters of other bodies in faraway places, naturally predisposed to . . . fieldwork . . . sweating through the interstices of . . . tea time. Edmund gives Fanny a horse; she rides passionately. They talk. Ethics and morality. Abolitionist inroads. Fanny is indignant about the source of the Bertram wealth. Black cargo. Sir Thomas leaves for Antigua to take care of business. The African lament does not return to sound through Fanny's gaze as she watches him go. The perturbation of her wrinkled forehead, sister, does not dissolve into a scene of a distraught ship, a silvery sea troubled by diving, tossed bodies. But she does stare, horrified.

"We all live off the profits, Fanny," Edmund says. "Including you."

Fanny looks helplessly about. Everyone else seems unbothered. For two years, they frolic, glad to be free of Sir Thomas. Patricia Rozema waves her hands toward and away from one another. They flutter like birds' wings; they ebb and flow like waves. Text Fanny rolls her black eyes. Time passes magically.

■

Through the enclosed garden of pressed glass, a waterfall gushes musically, and, nearby, a bronze Negro in livery stands proffering a green glass bottle of liquid. He stands amidst the monstera, the lady, the fantail palms of the solarium, while the Bertram girls competitively play the glass harmonium. Lady Bertram absently strokes her pug, murmuring, "I must say, the pleasures of life rarely transcend a moment such as this."

The Crawfords arrive, sexy siblings that set the Bertram sisters' mouths watering. Some denigration is in the offing, to be sure. Maria, at least, primes herself for adultery. The descent of quality; the blackening of the meat.

They play games, setting their sights on increased wealth through strategic partnership.

"And where is your brother Tom?" Miss Crawford inquires of Edmund, looking hopeful for a rich mate.

The younger Tom returns from Antigua, drunk and sullen.

"And how was Antigua?" asks Edmund. He left his father behind on the island.

"Ahh, Antigua! And all the lovely people there paying for this party."

Tom belches in Miss Crawford's face, slides from his mount, and nearly collapses.

Miss Crawford sets her sights on Edmund. Fanny Price is horrified; Miss Crawford is false. Mr. Crawford is a young wolf with tame eyes set on easy prey. Maria he'll have, but it's Fanny he wants. She resists. The young party contrives to press up against each other by staging a scandalous play, *Lovers' Vows*, while Mama lolls about and Papa is away. They stage the scenes in Sir Thomas' study, despite Edmund's imploring against it. Fanny, ever true to herself, abstains from acting and instead opts to prompt. To her dismay, Edmund is lured, despite all sense of honor, in his father's room by the captivating Miss Crawford. His nose is too open. Henry Crawford gets Maria up against a wall, while her husband, oblivious, yammers his lines. Miss Crawford pushes up, all cleavage and dewy eyes. Edmund licks his teeth. Jealous, Fanny runs off toward the stable only to find Sir Thomas returned home unexpectedly from the plantation. "How you've grown," he says.

He appraises her body with a glint in his eye. She is worth something. She blushes, a bit pleased, a bit uncomfortable. Does this denigrate, Fanny? Is the lament expected, a Malian echo, as your uncle's eyes roam over your form, trussed and draped as it is in sugar, cotton, rum, and blood? How that song of Africa haunts you; no one else can hear it. No one else wants to. What Sir Thomas does abroad is his business. Rozema persists, skillfully bringing slavery into the picture without presenting any actual black people. Fanny, apprehensive, mincing, trails Sir Thomas back into the manse.

∎

Meanwhile, the play continues its libidinous unfolding where it began, in his study. Sir Thomas' eyebrows roil in fury. His junior, Tom, emerges in blackface and tattered rags, holding a platter of fruit, his shirt open near to the waist. What can young Tom be in this moment, in blackface, that he cannot be otherwise? Exposed? A race traitor? Brave enough to revolt? What taboo does blackface give cover for? Sexual deviancy? Ah. Rejection of the Father. "You have blackened my name," says Blackface Tom, puppet to burnt cork's ventriloquist. "You have blackened me and I am no longer your son." We either read this between the lines, or blink it all away. What's it worth? Jane Austen shrugs. It not she do it. Sir Thomas roars. Young Blackface Tom flings the grapes at him and stalks out, jabbing obliquely at his father's hypocrisy. Sir Thomas quakes, flexing his fingers. *Where's my whip? Where's my hasenfeffer?* The remaining party gasps, stricken, not at Tom's corked-up skin, but at being caught in the act, the early stage of sexual scandal, under Sir Thomas' gaze, somehow also tinged with "it." Young Tom, washed up, runs off, continuing on the path of the debauched. Maria, denigrated by the taint of adultery, faces exile.

His blackface son's affront, the disorder on both his Caribbean and English estates, triggers something in Sir Thomas. Amplifies it. Makes it loud as the disembodied presence of an African voice, but not quite. Chattel on the homefront. He sets on Fanny, seeing to her comfort, that she has a fire in her room if not in her heart, that she is ready to marry, and join his investment in her to Henry Crawford's fortune. Is she out or isn't she? Sir Thomas throws Fanny a coming out ball. The party coyly dances in partnered lines, exchanging partners and knowing glances. The Crawfords hone in. Fanny will not marry Henry. Sir Thomas says, "Ingrate!" After all the time and money he's put into you, Fanny? Really. Edmund asks, "Would it really be so bad?"

"I'll not be sold off like one of your father's slaves!"

Instead, Fanny Price opts to return to her mother's home. In truth, she's given back.

Fanny Price's carriage rolls along the road, slowly, her white face in the window of the door, peering out intently. Follow her eyes and hear her mind for a moment. Our eyes merge. Our eyes are her eyes. See her memories. A far-off ship. She stares at the sea. It cries like a man, an African man, remembering. The cries rise again with Fanny Price's stare, as if her looking pulls the voice out from the unseen singer, out over the depths of the ocean and up the cliff face to her eyes. The wailing of the man's voice could deafen, depending on whether the attending ear seeks, or shuts. Such is the season, such is the style. The lament is brief, designed to sound like sudden thick mist, a rich *duende* troubling the water. Disembodied Salif Keita. The only African voice of slavery heard, and so easily missed. He echoes a remorse that reverses the wind.

■

Patricia Rozema waves her arm over her head. Seagulls wobble in the air then falter, turn into sketch paper torn from a book. Her cousin Tom's. Young Tom. Blackface Tom. Affected, speechless, fevered and near death Tom. He drew what he saw. Fanny Price stares and her forehead becomes a stage, her skin pulls back like a curtain of the future, of memory. Fanny Price sees Young Tom draw from memory scenes of his father raping a woman. Page after bird after woman after black woman struggling. The seagulls caught in wind, sucked backwards. The terror in their eyes. Seagulls screech. Her memory swirls in the air, the carriage wheels turn, this moment is brief, she is trundled back to poverty, Fanny Price, poverty amidst ships carrying gold, cotton, and slaves.

Among the ropes of port and barrel, Henry Crawford will come to court. The inference of wealth bobs along the sea, never entering her parents' house, but entering her, through ear and eye, *duende* and charcoal renderings. Memory bobs around her and there is the fire. Complaints of a tainted purity. Austen shrugs, staring above the lines, below the sea. Black women kick and scratch, locked in dust brown and gray, the undersides of seagulls' wings. Such visions. They topple and try to fly away. They're drawn back. Amidst rancid meats and fetid holds, Henry sends fireworks, releases a clutch of white doves in the air, his pledge of fidelity so juxtaposed with the shady dealings in the harbor. Henry Crawford, Love's gentle villain, walks along the sea, hoping to own a fair share of Fanny's heart, unaware that it is her ear he must contend with. The sound and the soundtrack of ethics and morality she measures his gait by. Can't you hear it? She says yes, Henry; she says no. One ear shuts and the other one opens. Fanny Price remembers Young Tom's black birds floundering, young girls on paper flying in the air, masts and sails.

She opens her mouth through the thin spray of salt water dashing off the rock, the flying gulls, the ship, the stare. Her eyes go blank. An African voice escapes from her lips. She no longer sees the ship, the ocean's waters. She cuts her eyes, looks straight ahead. The driver perched on the box snaps the reins and the carriage rolls away in smoky tufts of dust.

On a Sunday, two boisterous scenes take place on either side of a single mud track splayed with fresh road kill. On the right side of the track, affluent characters spill out from a church door, aware of only themselves and their finery. In their crowd, two old women kiss, the visible halves of their faces creating one whole. A man and woman talk into each other's mouths, their eyes shut down in self-satisfaction. Their small boy in rich coats, powdered wig and walking stick, dressed exactly like his father, glances indifferently at the mud track, the road kill in it. He doesn't see, just over the track, his poor counterpart bawling over a broken plate, or the girl crouched beneath it, eating the food that's slid off. On the other side of the track, a couple leans out of a tavern window, fighting over a piece of meat. On the other side of the track, a black man stands behind a white woman, openly fondling her breasts as she looks lovingly over her shoulder at him, both oblivious to the squalor all around. Over their heads, an illustrated tavern sign hangs: *Good Eating*, flanked by two teeth, over the head of John the Baptist on a platter.

WHILE LONDON BURNS

... VIOLET IS BLUE

We start with a quick montage. A young handsome in leather biker jacket, Danny, strides down the tube platform. Another young handsome, Sammy, is in bed with a naked American photographer. Handsome Danny in leather moves quickly. Handsome Sammy's lover tosses important papers around her posh loft. Sammy chases her. In a quick cut, we see his father somewhere in London fresh off a plane from Pakistan. The American lover, Anna, giggles. "Aren't you gonna go pick him up?"

Sammy smirks.

Danny is in his neighborhood now, where a woman is in her kitchen frying chips. Her son practices his trumpet. The American twirls; Sammy reaches for her. Not far off, the police rush up the staircase of the house where the woman cooks to trumpeting. They run up, landing to landing, covering each other, pistols cocked in the air. Sammy kisses Anna. The boy drops his horn and runs out the back. A cop kicks in the woman's door. The woman flings the hot pan of chips. The officer screams, scalded; his backup shoots the woman in the chest. She slides down the wall in a bloody smear. Outside, the crowd swells behind yellow tape. Danny approaches, cuts the tape with Swiss Army scissors. The people surge.

"What's this?" Sammy asks, pointing to Anna's buttocks, each tattooed with a blue "W."

"It's so whenever I bend over, it says, 'wow.'"

Now the title shot: *Sammy and Rosie ... Get Laid.*

This is the direction Stephen Frears takes the first ten minutes of his film. A young black man unexpectedly arrives at a scene where the black British woman who raised him gets shot, juxtaposed against an indolent young Pakistani caressing a white American's tattooed ass. Shot black woman. White woman's ass. Wow.

Danny, fine and young, rushes to the house now surrounded by the angry and curious.

He stands, rocking to lunge at the edge of a riot. Real fire, a real black woman, shot dead in her kitchen, by accident, by police. She's gone and this little world is about to burn. Danny Victoria is a man. He is called so. Hey Victoria! Hey, man! He is not a queen but of the queen. Of the crown. A winner unto himself, but he has lost something, someone now. And for love, for justice, he's at the edge of the boiling, scattering crowd, fists itching, not sure whether to leap and punch, hurl rocks, watch, or run. Danny Victoria hurls rocks. His sister sweet and not here. He runs off. He moves on to somewhere thought nowhere, nowhere but somewhere to be bulldozed, in a metal trailer shaped like a bullet, scrawled with marks of good faith. This is my home, he tells himself. He looks satisfied. A yard, a camp, a squat, a child he claims with care, kissing his woman good-bye, remembering his rage and promise.

Alternate take: His woman, let's call her Violet, fills the screen, her face is full of pain. She wasn't there at the riot's edge, but she knows about it, and knows they won't spend the evening together grieving and remembering the woman shot in her kitchen. She knows they won't light candles for her, she knows they won't be together to say a prayer. She watches him leave and recognizes the mark of the rose, of the crown upon him. She turns back to the trailer, and a friend calls to her, "Violet, Violet, man, don't you worry about 'im and 'er. Tend to your own garden."

Final cut: Danny's woman smiles and walks off without a word. What then, makes her presence necessary? There's seemingly no place for a straight black woman in this drama, except as a kind of ratio marker that makes Danny's non-single status equal to that of Sammy and Rosie's. He's . . . living with Violet. They're married. He even has a child, a baby boy, apparently; he never claims the child as his. Danny belongs to something (culture), someone (a silent girlfriend), a son. Child clamped to his hip, Danny Victoria strolls to a party. He'll meet Rosie, the cynical flower of the film, he'll irk Sammy, the lapsed activist philanderer, and take the flower back to his squatters' camp, currently threatened with destruction by developers.

"There was a time you would run into the streets if a black person was harmed!" Rosie bemoans to her Sammy. Rosie social worker. Rosie friend of an interracial lesbian activist couple hot on the trail of Sammy's daddy's human-rights abuses. And Violet? Unseen. Her silent comment, her role is to simply appear evolved on Rosie's terms, to give her man to Rosie's cause, carry the baby where Rosie has none, and appear completely unaffected by Danny's affairs, where Sammy is jealous. A silent study in contrasts. Danny is free. They, the white woman and black man, progress. Violet was never meant to bloom in their scenery. Rosie pontificates on the death trap of monogamous relationships. Violet is at the edge of the frame. Rosie's lips quiver hungrily. Violet and child disappear and there is Danny, beckoning.

"Would you like to come in for some hot chocolate?" The trailer will rock now, but later the camp will disappear into a memory of redevelopment, as will he, riding his trailer's back like a steel caribou. He steps lively, helps Rafi, an exiled Pakistani leader, a human-rights abuser, find his way through London's tubes to a long-forgotten paramour.

"My name is Danny. They call me Victoria if they like me,"

he tells Rafi. "Fuckhead, if they don't." Danny Victoria's body moves with the rocking train, he looks out the window, wondering where he might escort his own father to, toward love, to justice? Instead he is playing the good boy, the son, to Sammy's father, Rafi. He sighs. What he wants is family. What he wants is a home without wheels, a mother figure without a policeman's bullet in her chest. Rafi philosophizes about love and time and choices. They arrive at a spot where people stare, as if staring is the proper response to the fear of being beaten and robbed on a Tuesday afternoon. The long-forgotten paramour, Claire, wispy auburn hair and faded beauty, opens her wood-carved door, stares differently at Rafi. She never sees Danny Victoria, her other Other. She admits Rafi and closes the door. Danny Victoria disappears, goes off for a stroll in the tony urban village. Scales and vaults a high stone wall, drops like a cat into a lush garden busy with tenders. No one notices him. No one hears. He finds a flowered straw hat, walks easily about with it on, in leather jacket, close-cropped widow's peak. Sight blissfully, unbelievably, unseen. He returns to escort Rafi back, sans hat. Danny Victoria doesn't steal crowns.

On the edge rocking, rockers, silent, seen? Sure. The village burns. "No one understands what black people have to go through in this country," he tells Rosie. She strokes his bronze shoulder. "Oh I know, I know." You only know this, Danny Victoria thinks as he mounts her. A ragtag band, gray clad, move through these moments, in the Tube, along fences, like strong old twine binding fidelity to infidelity, Rafi's torture victims to Danny Victoria's police state grief, Rosie's blindness to Violet's existence.

To start, we see a black woman and a bullet through the heart; she gets lead. And all the white women get visibly, languorously laid. Oranges, browns, golds, and reds. Fire burning. Hot. Fire burns. Runs red. She raised him, the shot woman he rioted for, his lovely mouth curled about deliberately hidden teeth, the top lip, center, peaked to a suckable bud. The child riding his hip never speaks; neither does Danny Victoria, when the flower asks, "Is he yours?" In tight pants and synchronized cat-steps The Ghetto Lites sing a reggaenized "My Girl" in Thatchered twilight, while Victoria fucks the flower. Nobody understands what we go through, seen? She shot, they screw into injustice. The child silent, unexplained but claimed, riding the back of a gift.

Danny Victoria's woman, Violet, silently plays a belly synth, a deep song, unheard. She stands on the table. No one notices. She's not at the table with Rosie and the other women, drinking wine from jelly jars, complaining about men, and sex, and despotic daddies, showing each other how to put condoms on carrots. Violet, yard girl, what is your true meaning? Danny's virility? (Is he yours?) Whose child are you? Even the interracial lesbian couple, Vivia and Rani, get a hint of onscreen bed-time, Meera Syal as Rani in a nightshirt, lunging out of the covers toward the door as Rafi breaks in.

And you, Violet? Where are you now? Are you free to love, just not seen doing it? Just as Goncourt's Peau-de-Casimir was to be best friend in his title character Elisa's life, but ended up being a merely inexplicable glimpse of a black prostitute in a novel, were you too once a bigger idea on notebook paper: "Give Danny a girlfriend; create tension between her and Rosie; place couples in stark relief." Underdeveloped or cut out?

Meera Syal lunges at Rafi, threatening to castrate him. He runs off, falls. Cut. Rafi is shaken out of sleep, stumbles in a heap in Violet's yard, is recovered by his Claire. Danny Victoria is left, leaves to survive, sight unseen, hitches up, makes ready, some-where, as the bulldozers raze their squatters' camp, as Anna (wow) takes urgent photos. He secures Violet, and the boy in the trailer, beyond the frame. What made her necessary at all? This nuclear family moment. So outside the conversation. So exempted from sexual liberation. Her sex must act out else-where, where the roses have no eyes.

"Did you like each other?" Sammy asks with jealous fear, a new grief yet to befall them.

"He excites me terribly," Rosie tells her husband.

■

Violet, do you ask Danny if he liked her? Or do you just pack up the van? The ragtag band wends twine through chain link, linking justice to injustice to justice. In the end, of course, it's class that determines the lasting partnerships. Rafi hangs himself; Rosie and Sammy share grief and real feeling for each other, for once. Danny jumps and scales the moving trailer like a garden wall, Violet and the boy jostling inside, heading for another place to squat. The trailer a silver bullet dripping maternal blood. He waves good-bye to Rosie the flower, her fingers clutching chain link, his lovely lip curling, bud fades with a wave under the overpass. When the credits roll, the intimation of royalty and winning likened to his skin is lost. When the credits roll, they call him Danny. When the credits roll, Violet isn't there at all.

ARTIFACTS, V–II CENTURY B.C.

The Image of the Black in Western Art, Vol. I:
From the Pharaohs to the Fall of the Roman Empire

MENIL FOUNDATION

WILLIAM MORROW AND CO., 1976

Perfume vial in the form of a black woman's head.

Incense shovel with a Negro head attached to handle. The Negro's eyes are swollen shut, cheeks puffed with air, lips pursed to blow into the pan.

Gold filigree necklace with two carved garnet heads of black women forming the clasp.

Askos in the form of a child crouching beside a vase.
In the form of a child seizing a goose.
A naked child.
A Negro child.

Phiale decorated in relief with three concentric rows of Negro heads and one row of acorns.

Askos: a black woman dancing between a maenad and a satyr.

Balsamarium in the form of a black.

Kantharos: Conjoined heads of Heracles and a Negro.

CALIFORNIA NEGROES

Hebdomeros the Metaphysician, climbing a reverie, a route to fear, a man (is he a man?) witnessing a type of entrapment. It bears no relation to his. Once at the landing, he is struck by anxiety.

"Is it a man?"

Along the way up are columns of carved wood. Hebdomeros' master, Giorgio DiChirico, loves columns, loves to give life to seemingly inanimate objects in his paintings. When you turn your back, Hebdomeros, discarded storeroom mannequins savoy, have tea.

He encounters the figure and its use. To proffer a light to see his fearful darkness by, the figure's arms are raised over its head. It is bronzed, shirtless and comely. It is holding a gas lamp. It serves. He makes use of it. It is, Hebdomeros muses, a representation of a California Negro. Not unlike the Carolina lawn jockey, or the Moroccan penny gobbler.

He quivers upon seeing the figure, suddenly overwrought with sensations of going to a dentist, or seeing a doctor of sex diseases. The lamp, of course, is still. There is no explanation for this association. The figure, in the form of a bronze African, shedding light, is all it takes to send Hebdomeros' mind into the void. A sculpted, inanimate object, at the top of the staircase, at the end of one man's reverie, punctuates a personal history of worldly proportions. Hebdomeros' metaphysics, fossilized in the ceramic imaginary of emasculation. He touches the figure gingerly, leaving the residue of his origins, the sweat of surprise; the figure is cleaner than he suspected. The gas lamp in the figure's bronze hands glows like clarified butter.

This man is important. His jaw is smooth, as smooth as his distinction. He is a man of control. He remembers the weapons in the pockets of his athletic young companions, his companions who may notice the Negro-as-lamp but make no remark; the extra stores of munitions they carry bulge protectively, confidently, in their snug white pants. His manhood, while aging, is safe from denigration and the black stance at the top of the stairs, proffering light, a bared chest, and upturned eyes that submit to the fancy of any god who passes by. It does not blink at mad dogs. Strapping young men at the ready, his manhood safe and surrogate, now that it exists in relief against the figure, the general is primed now to encounter other, more fearful, apparitions. The Negro-as-lamp has lived here in the darkness of Hebdomeros' childhood dreams: a bear pursuing him through a maze of a once-familiar household, dreamscape of the interior, fits of panic and propulsion to flight (is he a man? can he love?), a dream that, like the figure, brought discomfort and illness to his lower regions.

Beyond it, through chambers of grizzled gladiators, a drawing room with a grand piano, there is a pianist playing, inaudible yet virile, the hammers of the instrument lined with felt.

"Nothing about him fit to be seen," the general says of the Negro-lamp, annoyed by the sudden appearance of people who trail about the piano as if hearing fortissimo, as if moved from within. The general is piqued; these people have no thought of guns! Not the war in the Transvaal, not the recent, undisclosed disaster at Martinique.

The Negro-as-lamp stands by the column, still as a sentinel. Hebdomeros dreams awake. A bullet. A bear. A devouring black fish. Rare white vessels that shatter, miraculously, without his touching them. We share this impossible power. We are related, not foreign, in this surreal space. What kind of man? Rueful, guilty, judging man, exploding with violence (a bronzed chest), desiring carnage of auto wrecks (ceramic thighs), fisticuffs in public crowds, a dentist with a drill (a buttery light), his sex rendered impotent or virulent. A poem. A myth. A landscape. A man whose trigger for staying erect we can point a finger at.

*To you a picture is simply a pretext for analysis. You wanted a nude,
and you chose Olympia, the first to come along. You wanted bright,
luminous patches, and you put in a bouquet. You wanted black patches,
and you placed a Negress and a cat in a corner. What does that mean?
You hardly know, and neither do I. But I do know that you have succeeded
admirably at doing a painter's painting, the work of a great painter.*

ÉMILE ZOLA TO EDOUARD MANET,
discussing Manet's *Olympia*

UNDER COVER

OF DARKNESS

Older Sister and Younger Sister climb the stairs of their childhood home. Younger sister flicks the hallway light. They drag
their feet down the worn wood floor, and force their bodies
into the too-small room they once shared as girls. The room
smells of their mother's perfume. Younger Sister sighs, flops
onto the twin bed, her head propped on pillows on the foot-
board, facing the old television. Older Sister turns on the VCR,
pushes François Ozon's *8 Femmes* into the machine, staring as
the black case of the tape is sucked down into the chamber.
The house creaks, pine trees scrape their branches against
worn shingles, still riled by the dregs of an April storm. The
closets hold decades of their mother's clothing. She takes her
space at the edge of the bed, her back poker-straight against
the headboard. She will not sleep tonight. The night is already
gone. The tape whirrs and wheezes.

The film begins. Its opening credits are reminiscent of
George Cukor's *The Women*. Instead of a parade of farmland
creatures, the sisters are led on a twirl through the garden.
Danielle Darrieux is a violet. Catherine Deneuve is a yellow orchid. Isabelle Huppert is a tight red celosia argentea, also

known as cockscomb. Emmanuelle Beart, the white orchid. Fanny Ardant, the red rose. Virginie Ledoyen, a pink rose. Anthropometaphorphism. Ludivine Sagnier, a young, lithe daisy fluttering in the breeze. Then the strings tremble deep, drop low, strike a chord of suspense, as if Joan Crawford's jungle red claws were about to slash through the screen, but that's not it. The vibrato of terror announces bright yellow petals surrounding an unfathomably brown center. The deepest notes produce Firmine Richard's name, quavering cursive white over the dark face of the sunflower, before it fades away.

Firmine Richard is Madame Chanel, the housekeeper. "Madames" were once cinema's stereotype for dominant lesbian femmes. In the space of her name, cathouse meets design house. Together they dress Firmine's body in old stories of race and sex and servitude, all with high style, under a mansard roof filled with hothouse flowers. Her dress is slate gray, domestic *haute couture*. Firmine is the shield that protects.

The sisters watch the flowers sing and dance their numbers to each other, as they applaud, react, respond.

"I hate that the housekeeper is black," Younger Sister says, glaring at Older Sister. "She has to take care of them. They don't listen. That's fucked up."

Older Sister makes an "Mmmm" noise, not for delicious, but to signal a very old yes. Their mother is very recently dead. Hours. She loved murder mysteries. And sunflowers. The sisters stay awake and the subtitles roll. Their grandmother cleaned rich people's houses in Jamestown during the week. Stayed away for days, while her children . . . While her children . . . sang?

Firmine strides from the kitchen, smoothing her white apron over her slate gray dress, cooing and cajoling for the girls of the house she keeps. "Her" girls, the Pink Rose and the Daisy. They are not dark and comely, but pink and white, forever presumed innocent. Their aunt is all irony, the sexually frustrated Cockscomb, their mother, the glib Yellow Orchid. Firmine the Sunflower stands tall and smiles, giving self-assured womanhood where there is only shrewishness, maternal warmth where there is only icy materialism. She stands firm, baking her girls brioche. The coals in the iron stove quietly heat and glow. Orange is a healing color. None of these flowers Firmine tends to have it.

But they sing about love and money and dance for the man whose eye they imagine to be constantly upon them. Just where is the source of all this passion, anyway? These women cannot be self-generating. As in Cukor's film, the Big Daddy of Ozon's 8 Femmes is never seen. He is a sleeve in a smoking jacket, a leg jutting from his study's polished armchair, a hand writing a check at his desk. He is nearly invisible, but evinced in each woman's actions. Except Firmine's.

■

Younger Sister eyes the Daisy bobbing on the screen with derision. She looks over her shoulder at Older Sister. "Are you freakin' kiddin' me here, or what? What is this?"

Older Sister shrugs, shaking her head, the thin rasp of air escaping her lips passing for a laugh. They look at each other gently. Older Sister's eyes drift slowly around the room. Younger Sister remembers something; her lips tremble, and she turns back toward the TV screen, resting her head on the pillow of her folded hands.

The scene is the morning after a night of many acts. Someone has killed the Big Daddy of the house. He's found in bed with a knife in his back. Whodunit? All the flowers gather round a glossy hardwood table, questioning, deducing, exchanging sideways glances, nursing suspicions, pointing the finger. At the mention of Big Daddy's sister, the Red Rose, sexy maid White Orchid and Firmine exchange glances.

Firmine lives behind the big house, in the hunter's cottage, where at night she entertains the Red Rose, a "fallen" woman who plies her wares on the wrong side of the tracks. In her hunter's cottage, Firmine is madame, silky, sprawled across her duvet in a black negligee, a cigarillo between her lips, mooning at her love. Red Rose sits perched on the edge of the bed, laughing from deep in her throat. They play cards; one trumps the other. Firmine's eyelids grow heavy with waiting for the moment when this innocent game will end, and another, more satisfying one will begin.

■

Beneath the sisters' bedroom is the basement, the laundry room, the coal stove, now cold, and the fourth television set, where Younger Sister once sat thumb-sucking and mesmerized in front of the screen, deaf to the bellowing of her own name. Where Older Sister was tricked by their mother to come down and watch *A Movie for a Sunday Afternoon* with her . . . and iron with her . . . and fold clothes, film after film, Sunday after Sunday. And here she is, home again and awake in the dead of night, hoping that this summons might turn out to be a ruse, that their mother might reappear, laughing as she steps out of hiding.

Estranged from her brother, and accused of being a money-grubber, Red Rose is a suspect in his murder. In the interest of justice, the sexy maid White Orchid outs madame house-keeper Firmine as a lesbian and Red Rose's lover. The girls instantly shun Firmine, stepping away from her in disgust. She looks to Red Rose for support, but the Red Rose averts her gaze.

"She is . . . a sapphist!" Grandmere Flower hisses at Firmine.

And only she. Somehow Red Rose is not a sapphist. Older Sister smirks. She too is a sapphist. She remembers the Southie Irish girl from high school who sat on top of the dryer in the basement, asking, *daring* Older Sister to give her pleasure. She hesitated then, immediately feeling that once the inevitable happened (word got out), and the finger pointed (sapphist!) she would never be seen in the pink-white light of innocence, of youth, as one of two equally culpable participants. Older Sister knew, as she bit her lip and made a move, that she would be seen as inexplicably dark and singularly corrupting.

Younger Sister dozes, wet lashes crusted with new salt.

Older Sister's gaze wanders away from the screen. She had recently spoken about this film to Anne, critical of how Firmine gets the short end of the stick throughout the film.

"What did he mean by all that?" she asked Anne, speaking of the director, François Ozon.

Anne waved her hand dismissively. "Pfft."

"Come on. He's deliberately using these stereotypes, the repressed lesbian housekeeper, the criminal lesbian madame, the loyal-yet-suspect black domestic, all rolled into one. All punished. He *must* be saying *something*."

"*Non, non, non,*" Anne insisted.

Older Sister bristled, but let it drop. This was to be cocktail small talk between strangers with a friend in common. Then Anne's hands waved more animatedly, as if orchestrating the *8 Femmes* soundtrack. Anne loved the all-star celebration of her country's actresses.

"And the trio of Deneuve, Emmanuelle Beart, and the picture of Romy Schneider, ah!"

No picture of France's equivalent to actress Madame Sul-Te-Wan falls out of Firmine's pocket in the midst of her playing the role of housekeeper, Older Sister thought. And *who* might that *be*, anyway? No portrait of Caty Rosier hangs over the fireplace in Firmine's hunter's cottage.

"I thought the film was just *lovely*," Anne had said. "And the bits with Danielle Darrieux were *hilarious*. It was special, rare, to see all of those women acting together."

Older Sister nodded, poured herself another glass of *velt-liner* and smiled, chewing a strawberry and imagining other possibilities for Firmine, ensconced as she was, as they *both* were, in the realm of other people's nostalgia.

I know this is not my future, Firmine thinks, but that somewhere else, at the edges of swamps and the mysteries of dead men, women grow true to their own desires. They know their worth. *Traversée de la mangrove.* There is another side, and a love that mirrors my skin, a child loyal to my blood, a sensuality that does not mock or damn, a vision that does not require my flesh as scrim. I cross back, to that other side, and stars are returned to my pockets to light my hips' curves with memory, with Time's continuous sway.

Younger Sister turns in her sleep, pulling the entire bedspread around her curled body, her hand close to her mouth. They have been returned to this position, fetal, blind, grasping, still dependent, suddenly alone, in a room too small to contain them. Older Sister watches the Pink Rose and the Daisy sit on the Daisy's bed, talking about sex, after they try to force Firmine to tell them all her secrets, she, the only one among them, it seems, who has ever known love.

Older Sister's eyes turn about the room still alive with her mother's scent. She cups her palm to her own forehead with force, as if to keep her thoughts from running amok, as if to keep her brain from bursting from her skull and splattering all over the walls. Love has two faces, she muses, one white, the other dark, each with an alibi. The mask of Art hides the devouring gaze, the vacant stare, the rapid blink in the face of History. The heavy cloak of Desire drapes over impassioned bodies as they crawl, panting with slick teeth, toward the border of Custom and Taboo. Dark shawls, pots of greasepaint, and discarded wigs litter this repressed landscape of sexual identity and moral culpability. Who is protected, in narratives in which certain desire is deemed perverse? Who shields, when taboo is tinged with the threat of social or physical Death?

"Have I ever let you down?" Firmine implores. "Without me," Firmine says to the Yellow Orchid, "your girls wouldn't have had much."

Yellow Orchid makes to slap her.

Firmine flinches from the blow, and turns to Red Rose, in a gesture of love, even begging forgiveness, though she's done nothing wrong. Red Rose rebuffs her in a bewildering act of violence. Older Sister leans forward. Rewind. Play. Rewind. Play. Red Rose grabs Firmine's hand, then Firmine is suddenly flung bodily to the floor, crying, disgraced not by loving another woman, but by having that woman violently deny her. She scrambles to her feet, her heel catches and tears the hem of her dress. Pink Rose suppresses a giggle. Firmine runs sobbing into the kitchen.

∎

Older Sister holds her nose, punches her pillows, then leans back against the headboard, eyes on the screen, intent on smelling nothing. In denying Firmine, she realizes, Red Rose, the "dark" lady from the wrong side of the tracks, uses Firmine's body as a shield. Firmine absorbs all the disdain and punishment for her love of Red Rose. Under cover of darkness, Red Rose runs away from any admission of sex with a black woman, but runs toward a very public display of sexuality, and taboo, with her dead brother's wife. Firmine, exiled and singing alone in the kitchen, tears streaking her face, maintains her balance throughout the farcical, musical murder mystery, though she's hurtling, being hurtled in each scene, from social to certain death.

"You need treatment," Yellow Orchid says to Firmine.

"It's the domestic's revenge!" Grandmere Flower huffs.

Older Sister's eyes burn. Younger Sister stirs, returns to sleep.

Firmine sings "so as not to be alone." She sings her song to no audience but the falling snow outside the latticed kitchen window.

Pour ne pas vivre seul
On 'sfait du cinéma
On aime un souvenir
Une ombre, n'importe quoi

Pfft, said Anne. Ozon meant nothing by the flow of Firmine's story. Yet Firmine sings that she's made herself into a cinema, a movie house, a place for other people's projections.

That, so as not to be alone, one loves a souvenir, a shadow, anything.

None of the other flowers look on with compassion as she sings of desire in spring and death and spring again.

Firmine's crucifix glistens. She is the diviner of truth, for it is she who discovers whodunit. And yet, she's still there, staring into Red Rose's flashing eyes, her treacherous, dimpled cheeks bridged by lips painted thick, hoping that there might still be a trace, a chance. . . . *I wait, I love you, so as not to be alone.* But instead Red Rose pushes up on Yellow Orchid, her own brother's wife, claiming, now, avowing, her same-sex desire, rolling on the floor with Yellow Orchid, kissing her, their breasts pressed together, for the eyes they imagine watching them, despite the eyes of the other flowers actually upon them. There is no disgrace, but a kind of mild wonder that passes through the room like hypocrisy, like the sun through the clouds.

Firmine bursts from the kitchen excitedly, the key to her redemption from social death on the tip of her tongue. "I know who did it!"

Blam!

Younger Sister jerks awake. "What the fuck?"

She stares at Older Sister, as if in sleep she might have changed the world. But the gray night is still the night; no one has returned. Not childhood, nor their mother's hands. Reality hasn't at last ceded control and left the world to the healing power of their dreams.

Younger Sister's glassy eyes follow Older Sister's to the screen, to where Firmine grimaces in disgusted shock.

"Oh, so she's shot now, too?"

"Mmmm."

There is no wound; Firmine has been hit, but no blood seeps between the fingers she clutches to her breast. Her eyes close slowly, in the fluttering throes of cinematic death. Then they flash open again, eerily undead, staring blankly out, as if transfixed by something, a vision, magic, a secret in the Continuum being kept from us.

It is as if the nurse were quite out of control. The other side of nursing, the opposite of the helping, healing hand, is the figure of destruction— the devouring predator whose inhuman and indifferent impulses pose immediate danger. Never still, always hungry, these figures are nevertheless seductive, elusive, and theatrical in their combination of power and deceit, love and death.

TONI MORRISON "Disturbing Nurses
and the Kindness of Sharks"

IN MELVILLE'S JUNGLE

> *There is no greater solitude than that of the samurai,*
> *unless it is that of the tiger in the jungle.*

BUSHIDO *Book of the Samurai*

The gait of the predator measured in matte fashion. Precise gray two-piece suit, brief gloss on black leather lace-up shoes, his hand reaching up in signature style to hone the edge of his brim. He's sharp, this samouraï, a tiger in his solitude. Camouflaged by surfaces, masked by color palette. He lies on the bed in his shirt sleeves, ankles crossed, cupping a hot Gauloises. The walls, sheets, floor, the caged bird singing contentedly, all complement in cool earth tones before the indirect glare of white light obscuring the outer landscape, filling the window frame like a blank movie screen. The only motion we see is a snaky cloud of smoke rising from white shirtsleeves into white light toward a black-shadowed ceiling.

Young Jean-Pierre Grumbach watched *White Shadows in the South Seas*, listened to the first words ever heard in film: "Civilization. Civilization," and decided that he too would adventure into the human landscape and create worlds. He also loved Herman Melville, and so changed his name to Jean-Pierre Melville. With his camera, he went on the hunt for bright beasts and shadowy creatures. And where he didn't find them, he made them up, like the quote from the Bushido that begins his film, Le Samouraï. Tripmaster Melville: His Fake Book.

Animal logic and suppressed narratives of adventurous desire. It all blends in Melville's jungle. The bird tweets periodically. Le samouraï rises suddenly, gracefully. In two steps he's across the room, hiding a mutilated wad of cash. He dons his Burberry, shakes out shoulders and sleeves, sharpens his brim at the mirror, and he's out. The bird says good-bye.

He stalks down the boulevard, selects an unlocked Peugeot. Sitting stock still, he methodically tries one forged master key after another in the ignition until . . . he's off! Le samouraï is neither smug nor self-satisfied. Prowess is its own expression. He remains pokerfaced, in control. At a stoplight, a creamy-skinned brunette in a similar *voiture* cruises up. She stares at him openly, all liner and lashes.

Am I your animal?

He looks her over, unfazed. She puffs out her lips. The traffic light turns green; he steps on the gas, hightails it through the rainy streets to his garage man, who silently swaps out the plates on the stolen Peugeot and sells le samouraï a revolver. He drives away to a posh apartment complex, goes in and stands at one door. Rings the bell. A honey blonde, Jane Lagrange, appears in a silk wrapper; he enters, she welcomes him into her arms. Jane Lagrange is played by Nathalie Delon, Alain Delon's then-realtime wife. They do not kiss. She is solicitous. He sits on the bed, checks his watch. "I was here from 7 p.m. to 2 a.m.," he says.

"No way," she says, "Weiner will be here at 2." Weiner the sugar daddy, the mark.

"So I was here from 7 to 1:45."

She looks pleased with that.

"I like it when you come to my house, Jef. Because you need me."

She gazes at him with a soft smile. He looks away. Gray hat on, trench coat collar up. Profile impeccable. She stares at him. He rises and leaves.

He enters a nightclub. The place is jumping. A beautiful young woman plays piano, jiving and smiling. *Le jazz hot!* Le samouraï heads straight to the men's room, puts on white latex gloves.

He strides behind the mirrored wall of the nightclub scene, down a long hallway of closed door, opens one, and fatally shoots the man behind the desk before the man has a chance to shoot back.

He turns, leaving, and walks smack into the path of le pianiste, standing elegantly in a long gown sparkling in the dark hall.

Their eyes lock. Close up.

Are you domesticated, or wild?

She stares at him, commanding the stage of the hallway, snug, sequined, stunning.

Le samouraï stares back. His mouth barely twitches, but he's been spotted! He disappears down the hallway, out of the club, and into the night.

Love has two faces, each with an alibi.

"He was here with me," says Jane Lagrange, to the cops. She loves Jef, but sugar daddy Weiner pays the bills. The inspector calls Jane a prostitute. The cops return later, toss around her lingerie; the Inspector tries to cut her a deal, tries to get her to turn on le samouraï. She won't budge.

"I've never seen that man before," says Caty, le pianiste, at the police line-up. Her voice comes in after she tinkled piano keys with long African fingers, her lovely Martinican face jiving, shoulders swinging, pursed full lips, now glorious teeth, flash of black lined eyes. Princess Tam-Tam goes mod. Again. Well you needn't. Her boss was shot by le samouraï. He shot from the hip, quickly and cleanly. Caty watched, aghast, as he stepped backwards from the scene of the crime. We don't see her watch. Her music covers for him. It began when their eyes locked in silence. Her voice.

"That is definitely not him," she says, eyes in close-up on le samouraï. Alain Delon stares quietly, penetratingly, questioningly back. Caty's eyes are glossy onyx, her hair sparkles, her limbs model-thin beneath plunge-cut sheathes. She cuts him slack to the police, says she's never seen him, when in the hallway they stared at each other, tiger and sleek housecat. Caty becomes the black question mark snaking through his mind. Everyone else is interrogated.

"He was here with me," Jane repeats. The blonde love. The devoted love. She too lies. (But who really saves you, Jef?) She cries. (But whose eyes do you recall?)

When he returns home, le samouraï's bird tweets in warning.

Caty, le jazz hot, is very cool, the star witness who also lies for Jef ... out of love? There is amour in samouraï. For her? Why would she lie for this stranger? Years later, she too is interrogated, by an off-screen female voice for Paris TV.

"Why acting?"

"You can't be a model forever," she says. "I'm twenty-four. I have a child of my own to support!" Caty strikes a number of poses: ingénue, gamine, le presence Africaine, in mudcloth cloak. She's a good model. Dandridge. Carroll. Berry. Look to the mark. See to her.

"You're very beautiful," Caty recounts the magazine editor's pronouncement as she flipped through Caty's book of headshots. "But you're *absolutely not* our type. *No one in France* can identify with you."

It is 1970.

But I am dark and comely, oh Caty, do you think, show me to the children of Césaire, the sisters of Fanon. Do they not live here? Can they not see?

The unseen female inquisitor's voice insinuates.

"With such a partner as Alain Delon, surely . . ."

Surely what? "A partner" says the inquisitor. Not "actor" or "lead." Instead Melville's barely submerged narrative of inter-racial desire is projected onto Caty. It's her reality. Her responsibility. So she expresses her gratefulness at being Melville's chosen. No one questions the reason. Pfft. It goes without saying. Critic Jonathan Rosenbaum calls Caty Rosier's le pianiste "a black angel of death derived from Cocteau's *Orphee*."

"I suppose you have an easier time with men than with women," the inquisitor persists.

"Much easier," Caty replies plainly.

"I'm not surprised."

Sisters of Fanon, where are you, cries Caty. Do you not rec-ognize this voice of Mistress, the wife of Plantation Pecoul's Master? Can you not see my face? My smile does not kill.

The phone rings. She ignores it. It's not her future calling. Caty glides across the nightclub stage to her piano; she wraps her tiger print fur around her shoulders.

The female inquisitor continues:

"So you're an actress by instinct?"

The eye of the camera closes in on Caty until she is only eyes, nose, and magnificent white teeth.

"*Peut-être*." She smiles.

Through the streets and stolen cars, the surveillance bugs in the curtains and the dragnet encircling him, Caty's brown face returns to le samouraï, returns him to the nightclub. We have to accept her "mythically and abstractly," says Rosenbaum, "not as any kind of psychological or spiritual entity," yet she is supported by the "poetry of fairy tales." Black angels of death need no motivation. They spring fantastically from our foreheads. And simply act! On instinct.

Whose animal is she?

After Caty's set, she and le samouraï get in her black Mustang. We see a Caribbean woman in a leopard fur coat driving an American muscle car named for a wild horse that's notoriously (mythically?) hard to break. What poem, what fairy tale is this? The seats, the steering wheel are blood red. Caty drives like she plays piano—she's not good at faking it. She takes le samouraï to where she's kept, in a mob nest, and she's evasive, enigmatic. Their feet sink into carpet as they dance around each other without making a sound. She wears a black kimono, swirls in a white fur swivel chair on the upper level of a white-walled duplex, covered in modern art. Piano music plays from nowhere. She stretches out, barefoot, on a platform bed covered in black zebra-print sheets. The boudoir becomes dark with hairy rugs and heavy wood.

Melville watches, perched, as if from an unseen balcony. As if high in a tree. His jungle scene is reaching its zenith. Now the shadow people who ordered the nightclub hit are out to eliminate le samouraï. She doesn't say she likes it when he comes to her house because he needs her. She says, "Call me at 2 a.m."

"Why did you say you didn't recognize me at the police station?" he asks Caty.

"Why did you kill Martey?"

"They paid me to. I have to know who hated Martey enough to have him killed," he says.

"Why should you care?" she replies.

Someone is trying to kill him now. He sits spread-eagled on a backwards Eames chair, chin resting on folded hands, gazing at her. The camera holds him. His blue eyes. Liquid? Repentant? Suicidal? Caty, what do you behold in this man, come to put his life in your hands, and do you want the responsibility of it?

The little bird tweets.

In his interrogations by the press, Melville says, "Filming is a tiresome formality. I prefer writing and editing, the inspiration and the finishing touches."

What is Caty's touch and what does it finish?

Civilization. Civilization.

Caty, lithe and lovely, steps down the stairs out of Jef's reach. She sits at her piano and plays. She is not to be attained. He thinks otherwise. His credo follows the cunning of the tiger. He runs his hand through her hair, lets it trail down her nape. The touch of the lover, the killer, savior and sinner; it's all on the same line. He stands behind her. Touches her. Her move away from his trigger finger is telltale, marked by desire. She moves into his touch before veering off again with a tinkling of keys.

Cut quick to Jane's. She answers the door before he's knocked. "Jef?" She "senses" his presence somehow, by ear or smell; it's unclear which. She's had trouble with the police, yes, but not because of him. Never because of him. She offers herself as the animal for him, no matter what. Her bed is covered in white fur. They stand in profile. He holds her by the shoulders. Squeezes. Gives her a peck on the ear, through her hair, turns to go. She stares after him. He doesn't look back. The door clicks shut.

Le samouraï breaks into the mob nest. Caty is not there. She too, like Jane the Fawn, is a kept woman. She is kept by the boss who orders hits. She doesn't act like it. Le samouraï kicks in the door, snatches the boss by his lapels.

"You got the four million?" the boss inquires coolly.

"Oui."

"Then you accept the contract?"

"Oui."

Blam! Le samouraï is faster. The mob boss falls, one bloody bullet in him.

He returns, again, to the scene of the crime, the nightclub. We see the gun chamber in his hand: six bullets. Cut. He enters the joint, resounding with jazz, a black jazz combo, and dons white gloves in full view. The bartender, who colluded on the original hit, backs away. Caty comes onstage in a white off-shoulder gown trimmed with gold. She sits at a small organ and plays something deep, tremulous. Jef walks deliberately to Caty at the keys.

"Don't stay here," she warns him, shaking her head to her own slow song, dolorous organ, echoing soul.

He pulls the revolver from his trench and points it at her. Melville the hunter darts his camera between their staring eyes, their faces filling the screen.

"Pourquoi, Jef?" Caty asks.

"I was paid to."

Her eyes widen. He makes to shoot; she flinches in fear. Le samouraï is shot by two cops in hiding.

"You had a close call," says one cop.

"Non," says the grim Inspector, flipping open Jef's revolver. The chambers are empty.

■

Caty's eyes shut in grief, or its double, ecstasy; her eyes shut with the shot. This is the moment, the clichéd ending. Le samouraï is dying. But she does not run to him, calling his name through a veil of tears. Her hand does not reach for her eyes, her mouth, or her heart, as she watches, as we watch, him die. She does not sign her body or the air with any gesture of love, or humanity. Through her, only death can be delivered. The finishing touch.

He stands in his study between table and chair, one hand resting
on a large, open book, the other gesturing behind him, toward the
bookcase, filled floor to ceiling with leather-bound, gold-foiled
spines. His gaze is penetrating beneath the soft curls of his powdered wig. He's smartly dressed in a buttoned vest, coat, trousers,
and stockings. Next to the bookcase, a framed scene, or a window,
displays an ambiguous landscape. At first glance a British country-
side is in the foreground, the closeness of wave-shaped hedge of
vegetation could be made to grow there, but then the eye is drawn
back into the distance and the images become both more defined
and less clear. The terraced sweeps of land. The faint outline of a
large house, long, white, tile-roofed caught in blazing light under
a tempestuous sky, the thin body of a palm tree swaying near it.
Francis Williams' head seems drawn toward that picture/window,
but his feet are planted face forward on the tile floor of his very
British room. His small feet and hands are quite noticeable, as are
the two globes adorning his study. One globe is placed on the floor
before the chair and the window to the ambiguous land, its detail
also indistinct, as it glows in the same bleaching light as the great
house in the distance. The other, a visibly marked world, sits on the
table, close at hand, next to his inkwell and quill. Between the two
worlds, Williams' gaze fixes itself on a place beyond our reach.

ANDRE'S MASKED BALL

The music points. Points to time, to skin, to sex. Is pointed. To blend. To stand out. Points at Edward "Ned" Kynaston, the last man to act as a woman on the London stage. He is its darling, Kynaston is, brilliant, demanding, a diva, emotionally attached to a blonde wig, clinging to a silk pillow smeared with mouth paint. Kynaston is white, in history, and in Jeffery Hatcher's play, *Compleat Female Stage Beauty*, but in this production, director Connie Crawford casts Andre Thompson as Kynaston. Ned Kynaston white theatre drag character meets black Jamaican Andre Thompson, gender queer in real life, but playing the role. They make a third body. Andre Kynaston is born. Andre Kynaston's specialty is Desdemona. Her Moor is theatre owner Thomas Betterton, a white in blackface. Classic. Death pillows and puns. How do you die playing a woman, as a woman? My Desdemona. Why is there a demon in your name and a Moor at your throat? "I die the best, no one plays a woman as well as I," Kynaston says, queen of all she surveys.

The music points at her with a white, a modern, an American finger: "Black!" Andre Kynaston is flying high, invited to court by King Charles II for dainties and fine ladies, then beckoned to dark corners for loving from the Duke of Buckingham. No matter the set or what role it plays, a bed is central to the stage. The ensemble cast is deliciously dressed 1660, shod in curlicues, garlanded, draped, wigged, flounced, and painted. Through interludes from stage left and right, wrought iron balconies and in the aisles, the ensemble vogues and vamps, lip-synching Whitney Houston's "I'm Every Woman" as flowers are flung at Kynaston's feet; her Desdemona dies *so* beautifully.

"Bravo!" Betterton bellows, agreeing then and there to give Kynaston, his demanding star, not only a share of the theatre's profits, but also final say on any casting for future productions. Betterton wipes the boot black from his brow, erasing the Moor from his skin, but keeping his eye on Kynaston. Maria, the theatre maid, takes the soiled cloth, regards the black upon it, presses it to her face. Ladies send fragrant notes backstage on fine paper to Kynaston's elation. Grinning, she adjusts her bodice, beckoning to sulky Maria for a hand. Maria loves Kynaston as *him*, not *her*. But Andre Kynaston just rolls her eyes toward more masculine types of adoration.

The world soars and surges, transformed by the Restoration. Andre Kynaston thwarts Queen Elizabeth's edict to rid England of the African likes of her. She is not an icon for fine tobaccos hung from creaking tavern signs. She is a star.

"Raah!" cries the crowd.

Behind the masque, she thinks, See this brown litheness, caressed, embellished, and so jeweled. My skin points to another music, in another place. My accent points, but I have no true speech here. This, my tongue, has no stage nor crown. I am not a drag queen, but dark, royal, and comely. LL Cool J's "Something Like a Phenomenon" pulses through her entourage. Andre Kynaston stalks the stage, her prowess doubly punctuated by the ensemble's pelvic thrusts. She twirls, feeling large, giggling between catty snarls. She's giving you realness, having a ball, and this London burns like Paris when she vogues. And yet the pointing never ceases. *What's that who's that why that's no woman why that's no man. What's in the pants the pants the pants.* Bawdy jokes abound: she's the cock of the walk. She's got a full purse in her knickers, of course!

News comes from across town that a *real* woman, a Mrs. Hughes, is playing Desdemona at a rival theatre, even though female actors are against the law. Kynaston is livid.

"A *woman* playing a woman? Where's the trick in *that*?"

Andre Kynaston always walks the public lanes still in costume, riding in carriages with ladies, exalted by powder, perfume, the power of working the stage, a territory demarcated by the power to control events as a man and act as a woman; a territory demarcated by his, *her* misogyny, and by never so dark a line as on the day of auditions at her, *his* theatre, when her black Desdemona's life is threatened.

Andre Kynaston's usurper-to-be is announced ("A Mrs.

Hughes to see you, sir"); daring to come to Kynaston's theatre, hopeful of support, encouraged by the king's top mistress, Nell Gwynne. Andre Kynaston snarls at the impudent servant's pronoun use, and makes for the stage, where Mrs. Hughes eyes him nervously.

Kynaston is haughtily dismissive of the woman, secure in his entertaining ascension, without a thought for the roles they play in his success. He ignores Maria's doting hands. He ridicules Mrs. Hughes' timid Desdemona; the gall of her to even try to play *his* role! He offers nothing constructive; he seeks to destroy. He heckles Mrs. Hughes and throws shade, quite full of the power Betterton, theatre owner, gave him: final say on new actors or productions. Did the woman *really* think he'd take her on as an *equal*? Andre Kynaston strikes a pose. The light catches the honey in his eyes. Andre Kynaston can, in this quiet moment, interrogate gradations of *realness* and womanliness, along the spectrum that he is the mark of. In this moment, we cannot ignore the darkness of Andre's skin, nor the glowing whiteness of Mrs. Hughes'. Kynaston dons wig, ready for the face-off of Desdemonas. But he's doomed for failure. *All the women are white, all the blacks are men, but some of us are* . . . not anticipated?

Andre Kynaston is a third body, created by brave casting, but did Connie Crawford see this third body coming? It was she who added the hip-hop soundtrack, the vogueing and signifying on black balls à la Paris is Burning. Yet in amplifying race and culture, by pointing constantly at Andre Thompson's skin instead of just letting him play the role, instead of just letting us forget his color, she created a racial subtext where there was originally only gender, and complicated the gender, by casting a black gender queer actor. The fact that we have been watching Kynaston's black Desdemona is elided. This third body, is it also ours, as we gaze, connect, project ourselves into his corset, into his suede breeches? Or are we only wall, bouncing Kynaston back to the stage, taking nothing with us? How are we to explain his presence? For we are not allowed to just let it be, even if we wanted to. The music points, to skin, to sex, to the myths we coddle or crush within us.

Andre Kynaston pauses, reflecting. Not a rival, this Mrs. Hughes. Talentless. Wan. She hates her. Yet she recognizes the threat. Kynaston and Mrs. Hughes exchange barbed quips like jealous schoolgirls. Andre Kynaston's black Desdemona is indignant; Mrs. Hughes shudders, but rises to the occasion. The entourage salivates, stroking their ruffles, taking it in. Is it doubled, the threat to both Andre Kynaston's manhood and her Desdemona? For our Andre Kynaston, darling of the stage, (wearing how many masks, now?) in the face of white female realness, white powder, and power, all of which she—and the play—refuses to reckon with. But we must. We see the racialized gender subtext as it's pointed out in the urban camp song-and-dance. Kynaston's challenge to the claim of the role of Desdemona shouldn't be affected by the race of the actor playing him (Kynaston) and her (Desdemona). But it is. *All the women are white* . . . Maria . . . Mrs. Hughes . . . Nell Gwynne. No non-traditional casting for *them*. Andre Kynaston's Desdemona snakes her neck and blinks saucily.

"Aaah!" goes the crowd.

There will be more diva for all and sundry, but later. The ladies demur; the Duke of Buckingham lingers with powerful admiration, stroking his ruffled belly. Samuel Pepys eyes it all, writes it down, claiming Kynaston the loveliest *woman* in the whole house. An unqualified compliment. Pepys and the ladies depart; Chaka Khan's "Sweet Thing" plays as Kynaston beds the Duke of Buckingham, blonde-wigged dome propped up by her favorite pillow.

When they have finished their stroke and arch and have scampered out, Maria strips the bed lovingly, angrily. Kynaston commands the stage, fixated on how he plays Desdemona's death. In her private moments, with Andre Kynaston gone, no longer understudy to her own womanliness, Maria, clutching Andre's pillow, does Desdemona differently.

How to be a man, then?

One must fall.

A candy-coated dandy, offended by Andre Kynaston's hauteur, hires thugs to humiliate her during her performance, then in a cruising park later, beats her severely.

Andre Kynaston, high on her talent, insults Nell Gwynne, King Charles' favorite mistress and Mrs. Hughes' good friend.

King Charles II changes the law banning women from the stage, to one that bans *men* from playing women. This is the Restoration. He wants to see some skin most unlike his.

The Duke of Buckingham marries, to Kynaston's ridicule, a highly placed lady with a bosom-rich purse.

Look now at Andre Kynaston, gay-bashed, lover-less, and banished from Betterton's, too, after all the law changing and flippancy toward the royal mistress.

And yet the public quietly admits what Andre Kynaston has always known: she's not good, Mrs. Hughes' Desdemona. She doesn't die well at all. But she is the first woman onstage to Andre Kynaston's last womanly man. The realness of whiteness is silent and sure, seen, girding the realness of woman.

Andre Kynaston limps along, clearing pewter from alehouse tables and begging for alms. How to be a man? Now that the black Desdemona, Andre Kynaston's Desdemona, has disappeared from view, now that Andre Kynaston is no longer the grande dame of the stage, but just a poor man, the soul and the hip-hop soundtrack cease altogether. The ensemble is restrained to plaintive string melodies. The point being now, simply and at last, Kynaston's being. The color of his desire is no longer conjoined, so thrillingly, so willingly, to his skin.

Mary J. Blige's "No More Drama" does not play. Gone are the blond wigs and garnet silk corsets. She becomes simply he, Ned Andre Kynaston, abject in homespun breeches.

He begs audience with the King, whose strumpet, Nell Gwynne, in revenge challenges Kynaston to be a man by playing a man, Othello, no less. And he cannot. He knows how to hate women, parody them, and keep them from the stage, but to play a man who loves a woman? A man jealous and afraid of having lost the love of a woman? Those feelings are hard for Ned Andre Kynaston to conjure. His Othello flags and falters. Nell Gwynne heckles him for not being able to deliver manliness on demand, just as he had once ridiculed Mrs. Hughes during her audition as Desdemona. Mrs. Hughes silently watches Nell have a go at Kynaston, but is discomfited by the scene, not avenged, but oddly saddened.

How to be a man? A woman? Ned Andre Kynaston's deep outrage sounds out. *This island, England, never called such, and that island, I am of, Jamaica, cannot speak for me, through me, here. I slip t'ru; I can't do this t'ing. No crown shall ring my tongue.* But your manhood?

Ned Andre Kynaston spirals down even further, prostituting himself in debauched pubs and bars, nasty songs hurled at his crotch, he lifts his skirt for paltry sums, until he's summoned to swallow his girlish pride and teach Mrs. Hughes' Desdemona how to die. His skin remains without music, layering the pointing, spreading it out along pores that pucker and rise with sudden chills. And that black girl who is not you now, Ned Andre, does she choke? Does she strangle? Run over your prone body blithely as a gazelle? And that black girl, who is not you, bound for Jamaica sooner or later from Africa, from your 1660s stance, can your vamp save her? Whose Desdemona will she be? And free? How to be a man, Ned Andre Kynaston? A black man? Or simply Ned Kynaston. Nothing but a man?

He ponders, simply, his role, his fate, gray and hungry in the indifferent London streets. Maria puts Kynaston up, ambivalent, but touched by his destitution. "Love me," she purrs. "How do you do it, two men? Who's the woman, who's the man?" Kynaston softens, and together they try to love, top, bottom, man, woman, expressed like so many confused asanas. Maria astride him, Kynaston grabs a wig and moans, guiding her hands to his throat. Maria is repulsed, spits at Ned Andre Kynaston, "I hate your Desdemona. You make her die so easily. And that's what's wrong with you. The woman in you is weak. Desdemona would fight."

Fully reproached and smothered by the subtext, the irony of a weak *and* black Desdemona, the transformation (of role? of body?) begins again. In a breath and a bellow, Andre Othello sires himself and, so humbled by Maria, agrees to coach his rival Mrs. Hughes to be a tough lady, though he still wants to kill her. He directs Mrs. Hughes, as her Moor, to play *his* Desdemona, and his power surges through the Jamaican rumble of rage set free from his throat. This, we are to understand, is not blackface but *black man*. He makes her crawl and mince and cower and show her love. He withholds all reciprocity, schemes, plots, and splits himself into his own Iago and Othello, Ned, Andre, Kynaston, whispering jealously into his own ear: *she is unfaithful to your vision. You are every woman, not she. Kill her! Make her die!*

Opening night, Kynaston's Othello is brilliant; Mrs. Hughes gives the audience authenticity, woman afraid, so beautiful. Oh, aaah! They respond, clutching their breasts, catching a view of hers. They step the paces, well shod and trembling to the near last, when Kynaston takes his chance at revenge, artfully strangling Mrs. Hughes within an inch of her life, arching his lithe brown body away from the talons that snatch desperately at his grimacing face, his taut ribcage. She snatches at him, Mrs. Desdemona Hughes does, she snatches at life, before her eyes roll, before her breath falters, before she goes limp. He rises, Andre Kynaston, Andre Othello, bellowing, tall, misled, destroyer, turned beast in Elizabethan anguish, then he commits his scripted suicide. He rolls aside as his Desdemona scrambles about the floor, gasping realistically, hand to throat, expiring, at last. *Kill her! Make her die!* One beat. Another. Then three. Mrs. Desdemona Hughes retches, and coughs. The crowd is still. Then she rises, shakily, bowing to sudden, deafening applause.

Displacing is a way of surviving. It is an impossible, truthful story of living in-between regimens of truth. The responsibility involved in this motley in-between living is a highly creative one: the displacer proceeds by unceasingly introducing difference into repetition. By questioning over and over what is taken for granted as self-evident, by reminding oneself and the others of the unchangeability of change itself. Disturbing thereby one's own thinking habits, dissipating what has become familiar and clichéd, and participating in the changing of received values—the transformation (with/out master) of other selves through one's self. To displace so as not to evade through shortcuts by suppressing or merely excluding.

TRINH T. MINH-HA "Cotton and Iron"

LOOKING A MAD DOG

IN THE EYES

Imagine a world of false windows, frames filled with still images. Unchanging windows. Imagine yourself. Picture yourself. Seen from the point of view of the unseen. The unknown. The unnamed. Your phone rings. It's the neighbor. You don't know the neighbor. You don't answer the phone. You know it's not your future calling. Your friend Anita answers. You feel . . . less despondent for a moment. You forget the final long night breaking up with Riccardo. Your mother never asked about your long face. You're used to her. Not asking. About your face. About you. Sleepless. Restless.

"I'm not tired," you say. "I'm disgusted and confused. There are times when holding a needle and thread, a book . . . or a man, is all the same."

Anita listens. How to make your presence felt, or your erasure clear?

"What can I say," you say. It's all the same. You turn the lights on, then off, and darkness deepens, or grays. You hold a black shawl up to your face. You become a swathe of darkness with white hands. Anita sighs. You watch her answer your phone as you are watched from afar. A Kenyan girl, eyes downcast, hand on hip, looking down in your direction. Exquisite. Inconceivable, in this place.

"She wants us to come over," Anita says, her hand over the receiver.

"But I hardly know her," you say.

You're listless. Anita seems to care. You don't tell her about meeting Alain Delon at the stock exchange. What's to tell? The phone startled you. You feared it was Riccardo. But it was your neighbor, your neighbor who is a stranger to you. Your feelings back up. You rush with Anita to the balcony and look up, your silhouettes bent over the rail. You're small, becoming smaller, like thickly inked stick people. The adjacent silhouette above you, the neighbor, impervious, far away from your eye. You race Anita down the corridor and up the stairs to the neighbor's door. The Kenyan girl stands, fully aware. She's pressed against the wall, unmoving. From behind the wall, from behind the Kenyan girl, Marta, the neighbor comes into view, opens the door, lets you in. You brush past the Kenyan girl. Her skin has lost some of its glow from so much contact. Her skin has the feel of heavy black paper, a souvenir poster, placed to stand in the space over the balcony. She only *seemed* alive, obscuring the details of your reality and looking down on you. This is Michelangelo Antonioni's L'eclisse. And a sign of things to come.

■

Anita drifts straight to Marta's bed. You comment on its large-
ness, its firmness, its placement on the floor. Marta's is a set-
tler family, with a farm in Kenya. Her coffee table stands on an
elephant's foot. You trace its toenails with your index finger.

"That's Kilimanjaro," Marta says, pointing.

"Well, well," you say. You look at the pictures of Masai girls,
of Masai warriors. "The snows of Kilimanjaro."

Where before there was utter silence, now there are drums
to accompany your gaze. Drums for every blink of your eye.
Drums in the cut between your white self, seen, and this other
sudden presence. The not-you. Cowbells and blackface. You're
magically done up in coal dust, gold coils around your neck. Is
that you? It's been said that Antonioni inserts himself into the
mise-en-scène of every one of his films. Where is he here? In
the long wood carvings on the shelf? In the animal skins?
Might we find him, even now, somewhere in the smut on your
face, the smudge of this imaginary Africa?

Anita holds an image of a Kenyan woman up to your face.
"Look like her?"

"*Identica.*"

Unseen men chant in an unidentified language. No record
plays; tribal sounds simply fall out of the sky. You begin to
"dance." Tippy toe hip thrusts and jutting buttocks. Shrieks.
Anita stands by a skull. She is strung with beads and heavy earrings.

You are outlined against the white walls. You grab a spear. Marta, in her floral housedress, rises irritated from her rattan perch. Neither of you notice the dark silhouette following her, surrounded by walking sticks, bones and jars. She stares at you. Your "dancing" stops. Scolded, you and Anita flank each side of the fireplace like enchanted statues.

"That's enough," Marta cries. "Let's stop playing Negroes."

You pout, looking busted, and take the gold coils from your neck. Perhaps this play is not new to this moment. Marta is cranky. She cannot sleep when her husband is not around. The camera rests on tusks, horns, and other adornment. Behind the bed a floodlit reproduction of the Serengeti spans the wall. They still sleep, Marta and her husband, in Africa, with Africa, with a Kenyan girl guarding the door. Is it here that we find the man in the mise-en-scène? Is it afterwards, on the bed, as you wipe bootblack from your arms with a towel, and the wine is passed, that you look for yourself?

"Sixty million blacks want to kick out the whites," Marta says.

"And it's about time," you say.

"They have guns now. Only ten of them went to Oxford. The rest are like monkeys."

"They must be charming monkeys," you smirk, looking at Anita. Anita looks at Marta.

"They finish the first grade and think they are leaders."

"Then let them finish the second," you say.

"What?" Marta says.

Is this where Antonioni secrets himself? Not in talk of Eritrea or Dodecaneses, where Italy did its colonial business, but in talk of the British colonies? Or is this a simple homage to the complexities of Hemingway?

"Why did you go back to Kenya to have your baby?" Anita looks at Marta earnestly.

"It's my home. And it's a very modern clinic."

Marta stares off at the pictures of Kenya on every wall. It comes back to her, comes to life, and you quietly watch her revel. Something in you prevents further speech. Now you've returned to the moment. Riccardo is gone. Three women on a bed. You're the only one who's still single, still lost in the jungle. The room becomes bright again. Each of you looks in a different direction. We see your backs, sides, profiles of evasion. From somewhere outside, there's a heavy metallic clang.

"The dog! It's gotten loose!"

"How?"

And so you flee now, as you soon will into and out of the arms of Alain Delon, into the isolated night, scattered with dogs and streetlamps. In the jungle night, you tell Marta, things just unfold on their own. It's much easier to be happy. But here, here in Rome. It's much more difficult. Even in love.

A dog runs past. You lurch after it, the backs of your legs white batons flashing against the deep of evening, the all-consuming . . . leaving only a bit of light to see your confusion by. You run into the darkness calling, "Zeus . . . Zeus!" scrambling desperately after the dog as if the night, coupled with your labored breathing, might truly transform it at last into your god.

"The bust-size figure of the negress is elegantly dressed with a feathered turban and bejeweled with earrings that would have activated an ingenious clock mechanism. In pulling the right earring, the hour would have appeared in the right eye. A pull to the left earring would have indicated the minutes in the left eye. A model of this clock made by the clockmaker Furet was delivered to Queen Marie Antoinette at Versailles. Before its delivery, the clock was exhibited in Furet's window shop where flocks of passersby stopped to contemplate it in awe."

PORTRAIT OF A LADY

It's 1762, and we find Queen Charlotte Sophia, resplendent in a yellow bone-waist gown.

She's seventeen, a queen, child of Mecklenberg-Strelitz, and she speaks no English. She stares out, away, beyond, talking to herself, the landscapes, someone in her mind who speaks her language. The new principal painter for the family arrives; she turns from her reverie to face his inquisitive eyes. His smile is faint and disconcerting.

"Herr Rrahmszee," she says, and stops.

He bows, but too soon he returns to her face. He seems to be looking for something, searching. After all, he's somewhat of an abolitionist, this Allan Ramsey, and he's heard the poem of her wedding and coronation: *Descended from the warlike Vandal race / She still preserves that title in her face.* . . . He begins his underpainting. Underpinning. Allows her nostrils to gently explore the plains of her face, her tawny hair its particular heft and curl, the hue of which he extends to slightly tint her skin. He paints, ever so delicately, Africa as he sees it sleeping in her. It's what the times call for. He paints her shining scepter, the spotted fur of her crown. Months later, the work is done; Queen

Charlotte is quite pleased, as is King George I I I. They keep the portrait as a treasure in the Royal Household.

It's 1789. The Queen is distressed. Her king is babbling at the moon. Poor George. Poor her. All their flair was for repression; so dull. Now insanity has set her George free, but her? She's pressed to sit for yet another portrait; this near number seventy now. She barely recognizes herself between them all; her lips and nose vary so. But they are hers. The portraiture will hide her African features, but history will not. Some will dig to show it up. She passes through the room, glowing, light, honey-like, in silk robes, her thick tawny hair pulled in tufts of ringlets. She dislikes the dark wood of the room, but the painter insists. He dresses her in blue. She wants more bronze, richness. She strokes the clock, the early gift of French time-makers.

"Your Highness," says the painter. "I'm instructed that your portrait is not to show . . . your unfortunate Moorishness."

She considers her nose, so often remarked upon at every occasion. Even her personal physician says she has a "true mulatto face."

"Yes, yes, well . . ." She drifts off, then turns to him, smiling the wan smile of royalty. Hers, despite her African ancestry and her husband's insanity, is considered the most lifeless of monarchies. Queen Charlotte Sophia, dedicated to the domestic sphere, had fifteen children.

Whatever excitement remains of the vandal race, thinks the painter, must need by now scant restraint.

"With your forgiveness," says the painter.

He reaches out to the Negress clock case on the cherry demilune and pulls its left ear. The queen's eyes turn blue. He pulls the clock's right ear, and Her Majesty's hair refines itself, smoothes, darkens. Last, from the turban of the Negress clock, he pulls a feather, and waves it before Queen Charlotte's face, her neck, then her hands. A faint crystalline haze comes over her, her nostrils constrict noticeably, and then . . . she pinkens.

What holds civilizations intact? The presence of apparently voiceless Others, "thoughtless" Others, powerless Others, against which the Law, the Main, the Center, even the Diffusions of power are defined.

RACHEL BLAU DUPLESSIS "For the Etruscans"

THE HEAD OF THE MOOR

The biographer/narrator in Virginia Woolf's novel *Orlando* begins her "research" into Orlando's story as a joke, a joke that begins,

> He—for there could be no doubt of his sex, though the fashion of the time did something to disguise it—was in the act of slicing at the head of a Moor which swung from the rafters.

The joke advances into a spell, an incantation into the black arts. What constructs a man's prowess, a woman's delicacy, or a narrative of wealth and sexual transgressions? The biographer is one of many guises covering the real face, the voice of Woolf herself, as she revels in her love for Vita Sackville-West, and her fetish for the complexities of noble pasts. She speaks to, about, for, and through. Still.

I write to Esther and ask her what she thinks. Esther is on a first-name basis with Virginia Woolf; she has an affinity with her Virginia, the depths of which have yet to be plumbed. At the surface, though, is her near-total recall of her Virginia's letters, books, and those of the lovers, husbands, and friends in her Virginia's world. Esther says *Orlando* is a critique of Empire, a parody of a certain kind of biography, and, most importantly, a love-letter to Vita Sackville-West. Woolf apparently believed that a human being is made up of thousands of selves existing across time and space. Woolf writing as parodist, lover, critic, self, and more. But there's much in *Orlando's* fabric that Esther's deep knowledge of her Virginia cannot account for, the racialized darkness throughout, exoticized, yes, but not interrogated, over time and space, between thousands of selves, writer, critic, reader, admirer, gatekeeper.

What we have is Woolf's *then* in our *now*. Parse the registers. The cusp between them dark as oil, snaking and slick, cleaving the land with a liquid that moves dusky beings on ships and barges from one country to the next. We talk to the page, the screen, or the scrim of imagination. How to be a man? A woman? See to the mark: there, there, and there. And we are? Where? Reading the figures of time, image after image after image.

We add our voices to history and bodies move across time. Lineage, not forgetfulness, is spoken and does define and demarcate "us" from "them."

Orlando stalks the attic, invisibly crowned, the violent mist of his bloodline curling around his head, a coronet, violet eyes intent on the makings of manhood. He strikes to a beat. Once. Twice. Three guineas. And one Moor whose vanquished head swings in the house of the lord who struck it off. The look on his face belies nothing but purity, beauty, youth, and wealth, all bequeathed from battlefield swordplay. Onward Christian soldier! Lovely legs, clad in tight leggings, the calf encircled by garter, his lithe tongue crowned. The basis of empire. The primal scene. Seen? The Moor's head swings, decomposed, sparsely haired, dark as a coconut or an old football, but still a Moor. A trophy. This is the battle to make boy man.

The music points to the beat of Orlando's swing. Man. Not man. He's surrounded by beauty, his own and his forebears'. His violet eyes glitter with peacock and gossamer, rosy lips and river waters, the green grasses of ancestral memory where grandfather slayed and slew, on the arras where elephants returned annually to rest near their mothers' bones. Where elephants return on the heads of coins, under the bust of King Charles II. Orlando teaches himself chivalry by letting the head drop to the floor, then stringing it up again, almost beyond the stroke of his boyhood sword. It began as a joke. The head swings from the rafters, a Moor, of rulers and royalty, but vanquished nonetheless. "All ends in death," Orlando says, his breeches filling and lengthening. Vita, vita, pulsing through the blood, rising to the occasion.

The head of the Moor swings to the beat of Orlando's love. Royal figures flutter their eyelashes in his direction. "All ends in death," the sullen young male intones, ruffled and taffetized, bejeweled, dreaming of love amidst the leopards and coronets. And love comes, in the form of Sasha, a Muscovite princess, eastern, ebony-eyed, sable-haired, her sex sealed with tallow to keep out the chill. He spends his time by the frozen river, eyes lit by bonfires. He falls in love, falls through velvets and brocades, falls through the ruff and tumbles acrobatically about, his pants, his mind, his future, secure. She hangs her darkness over her, musky and foreign, and at first he is unsure of what's under her skirts. Will he slit the fabled tallow sealing her sex with an aristocratic thumbnail? Peel back the lips of that other language between them?

The darkness of the Russian babe, the inky darkness of the London sky, Orlando's desire, rage, manhood, swing the spectrum of darkness. She gave off the scent of desire, flashed her eyes but said little, said not, "O, my fine boy, I see the rich dark earth that mingles in your heritage." Said not, "I am not your wanton, but dark, royal and comely." And he stayed by her silence, by her side, in the night, wanting.

On their last night, before the flood that occasions his meltdown, they watch a puppet show in a miniature theatre. A lady puppet in white laid out in all splendor, surrounded by white gowns like the wings of the cherubim, and a dark puppet, a Moor, hovered above her in a frenzy Orlando saw as his own. As the Moor puppet kills the lady puppet, Orlando's violet eyes burn through the scene. He sees himself killing Sasha

with his own hands, his manhood again mingled, offset, in relief once again.

Orlando loses his erection as well as his position at court with
the King. He falls into a funk that smells like molting chin-
chilla, like flesh decomposing, a heart fissured in release of
nightcrawlers, subterranean vapor. In his fall, Orlando pulls
the head of the Moor down with him, or so the biographer
says. Or the writer pulls the Moor down with Orlando, trans-
forming the head from "Moor" to "nigger" as Orlando drops,
head in hand, to his heartbroken knees. The language shifts its
weight from critique of Empire to a simple slur. Who is being
called so? The Moor, or Sasha the dark Muscovite princess
who broke Orlando's heart? Or some real person upon whom
Sasha is based? It's hard to say, with so many selves populating
Woolf's prose. Rows of white figures raise and lower black
masks to their faces, one after the other, over and over, across
time and space. Perhaps Woolf, in her guise as someone else,
in the register of some other power not hers (parody of biographer, parody of power?), reduces the Moor to a moor to a
nigger as an act of ventriloquism. It not she do it? Then who?

Can you explain this?

Meanwhile, Orlando drops deeper into blackness, at Black-
friar's Inn, where Sasha stood him up, amidst grayed-out men
begging for alms, clearing pewter from the grimy decks. Is this

what made "nigger" necessary? And if one was not versed in the Virginia-Vita code of lover's talk, and letters between the inner circle, if one is not clear on logic of Virginia Woolf's empire bashing, was not then, in 1928, and is not now, whatever the now may be, what then, is the importance of the scenes we're given?

Consider this:

"The black page at Knole," wrote Vita Sackville-West, "of which there had always been one since the days of Lady Anne Clifford . . . had always been called John Morocco, regardless of what his true name might be." The 1613 register of those who served Vita's ancestral Long Table in the Hall lists one "John Morockoe, a Blackamoor" at the very end. Vita mentions, without much inflection, that a house-steward once killed a black page in the passage.

So perhaps Virginia's license to reduce Moor to moor to nigger simply exposes the reality of thought between herself and lover Vita, among many of those of her ilk. Ancestral thought? It wasn't "the times"; it was *them*. So what in Vita is Woolf *really* celebrating, fetishizing in *Orlando*?

In the shadow of a giant black hairy rabbit encrusted with dung, Orlando stands, desirous, contemptuous, for love has two faces, one white, the other black. The servants and the nurse, the housekeeper and the chaplain all get involved in trying to raise Orlando's spirit by stroking his ego in loud voices. Even the Blackamoor Grace Robinson takes part, showing all her teeth in a broad grin while praising his Lordship. (But whose head is that in the attic?) The biographer, framed in white light, raises the hirsute wooden mask to her face as Orlando whisks himself out of the doldrums and off to Turkey.

Memory, the hussy, brings tears, and Time sweeps over Orlando, a dark hand before his eyes, turning skin to dusk, the primal, prowess, animal gentility, Orlando's legs racing through wood and country, the arras of ancestors, Moors, and falling trees. He must have some secret connection to the dark gypsies, though they have no word for "beautiful." But King Charles' strumpet, Nell Gwynne, so loved the sight of Orlando's legs she begged good Charles to elevate the boy to the highest rank in the peerage. But that is only a rumor. As ambassador to Turkey, he eats well, and thinks not again of Moors nor Muscovites. The biographer is delighted. He buys a fine herd of goats. The gypsies chide him, surely, but yet and still they have their use, in contrast, in relief. What gaiety! Will nature make a man of him yet? Sure, there's the rumor of the dark woman lover of Orlando's, of Vita's, forebear, the one who nearly compromised the Sackville wealth. But Orlando is placed in darkness; Woolf likes to flirt with his, with Vita's being of darkness. Orlando stands out. The point of difference, manhood, virility, Empire, notwithstanding (how can we withstand?) is sexual. How to be a woman, who loves women, without making that love (it has two faces) "dark"?

■

122

Vita's savagery is to Esther's Virginia a positive term. Esther says it makes a difference. There's something still a bit stinky about this tar-brush business; much as Woolf's oeuvre points to her radical thinking, her feminist dialogue, *Three Guineas*, is nonetheless titled in the currency of the British slave trade to make its points.

Man-Orlando is cloaked in darkness; Orlando-woman will see the light, without a backwards glance to what that woman-hood (Moor, nigger, Empire) is built on. What multitudes it contains. Thousands. In time and space.

What do you see in this?

Orlando loves and his love transgresses, transforms itself and him, before the eyes of Grace, the servile Blackamoor, under the kissing lips of a Turkish gypsy, Orlando's inner blackface points to its kin, and his, and in the flame of a native uprising, he strikes a pose, and falls beautifully to sleep. Other! As he . . . becomes she.

One might say that immensity is a philosophical category of daydream. Daydream undoubtedly feeds on all kinds of sights, but through a sort of natural inclination, it contemplates grandeur. And this contemplation produces an attitude that is so special, an inner state that is so unlike any other, that the daydream transports the dreamer outside the immediate world to a world that bears the mark of infinity.

GASTON BACHELARD "Intimate Immensity"

THE PROBLEM OF DIDO

Somewhere, in the Continuum of our now, two girls sit for a portrait on their uncle's massive Kenwood Estate, along the grounds of Hampstead Heath, London. The painter, Johann Zoffany, places one cousin, Lady Elizabeth Finch Hatton, gently on the right edge of a painted wood structure, a trellis, a high-backed bench. Her dress is a corseted pink and white affair, featuring a triangular bodice of white lace atop pink silk brocade, covered by a thin layer of gossamer gloss.

"Pretend to run," Zoffany says to her, "as a lady would run." The young Lady Elizabeth, negotiating around the apparatus of her skirt, attempts to bend, pressing a knee against the fabric of her skirts. It's an awkward stance, not fully seated nor standing. It's a kind of lunge.

"I'm not . . . comfortable," she says irritably.

"Yes. And . . . ?" Zoffany begins, conducting her expression with an upward sweep of his hands. Lady Elizabeth faces us. Her eyes are large, brown, and soft, her hair adorned with tea roses at the crown. Her cheeks pink, her lips red, her chin slightly cleft, the double strand of pearls around her neck nearly blend in with her skin. Her right hand holds an open book in her lap. Poetry. Or myth.

"Now here." He takes her right hand and tucks it to rest on her cousin Dido Elizabeth Belle Lindsay's crooked elbow, not closely, but at arm's length.

Zoffany places in Dido's right arm a shallow bowl of peaches and figs with sprigs of new oak and grapes hanging over the edge. "What am I to do with this?" she asks.

"Just *hold* it," the painter responds impatiently.

Dido glances at Lady Elizabeth's book, then back again at the bowl of fruit in her hands. She pouts. Zoffany's hands orchestrate Dido's body into a stride, which is easier for her than it was for Lady Elizabeth. Dido's dress is nothing like her cousin's; it is without bone, corset, or triangular bodice. It is devoid of white lace or even a hint of pink. Dido's dress is of a satin pajama variety in silver gray, with a waistline and drape reminiscent of Greco-Roman sculpture. Her skirt is without the layers of petticoats the day required to hold fabric away from flesh, as was the fashion for ladies, at least on the bottom. Dido's dress clings indecently to her form, the shape of her legs and backside visible under her dress. Zoffany produces a beaded turban from his trunk of notions, of the kind often seen in Orientalist paintings by Delacroix. Young Lady Elizabeth gasps; Dido makes a sound of resignation. The painter covers Dido's thick, braid-coiled chignon with the turban, its one marabou feather punctuating the top of her head, pointing down at her, exclaiming. Last, he waves his hands about her deadpan face in an upwards motion until her lips curl up enough to show her dimple. Zoffany takes her left hand, and puts her index finger impishly to rest beside her mouth.

"You certainly look silly!" Lady Elizabeth says indignantly, looking first at Zoffany, then at Dido, who returns her cousin a knowing look. Then they burst into laughter. Zoffany is amused, exasperated, then stern. He hasn't much time. Giggling, the noble pair manage to pull the painter's contrivance back together, their eyes still gleaming. Dido looks mischievously at us. Her eyes are large, brown, and soft, her hair concealed beneath a feathered, beaded turban. Her cheeks pink, her lips coral, her chin slightly cleft, the single strand of pearls around her neck stands out away from her lovely brown skin.

Zoffany hurriedly sketches the scene. Their gaze impresses upon his charcoal their similar faces, and yet the narrative he constructs contradicts itself. Lady Elizabeth could be touching Dido's arm affectionately, or pushing her away. They might be equals in all things, but they are dressed to show marked social difference. It's an ambiguous stance, often interpreted as loving, this portrait of interracial family during the time of England's colonial, slave-trading dominion. Beyond them, a bridge over water, a hillside, the tiny detail of London in the distance. Dido does not appear seated at her white cousin's feet, but a sign of true affection between the two is a bit hard to come by. The space between their bodies, measured by Elizabeth's outstretched arm, helps us read the myth of it. Faraway, so close.

■

There is another story of a young girl from Senegal, Ourika, who was adopted by French nobles and raised in splendor. She died, it seems, from unknown causes (despair, out of the kumbla?) at age sixteen. What survives is Claire de Duras' written, fictionalized version of the tale, Ourika, which she learned and often told to entertain her guests. Ourika is adopted by one Mme de B. of France and raised as a young lady of French society, albeit a sequestered one, where only family and friends delight in her company. Ourika was raised to feel herself equal to her brother and others. She's not conscious of her difference. But de Duras, through the mouth of Ourika, speaks the code to her audience:

"Dressed in oriental costume, seated at her feet, I used to listen—long before I could understand it—to the conversation of the most distinguished men of the day."

Ourika doesn't dress in the European fashion for company, nor does she sit in a chair, a self-contained subject. Instead she's perhaps garbed in satin harem pajamas and a turban, on the floor at her benefactress' feet. A pose of gratitude worthy of a. . . . Chevalier de B. had rescued Ourika, a toddler, from slavery, as she was being taken aboard a ship. Her mother had just died, that minute, hour, day, nameless, faceless, graveless. Ourika has no memory of anything but the lavish estate she lives on.

■

It's 1779. The Queen of England has unfortunate Moorish features. It's a time when many now living in London believed there were no Africans present there. No slaves. And a time when black people are snatched from London's streets and "returned" to slavery in the West Indies, whether they'd known it before or not. Dido knows only Kenwood, where she is kept safe. She is twenty-four years old. Zoffany finishes his studies for the painting and at last the ladies are free to go. Dido goes to her rooms to change into something proper, leaving Zoffany's costume to a servant for its return to him. She hurries down the back stairs and down the rear hall to her great-uncle's study to take his letters for the day. Her great-uncle is William Murray, known throughout British society, and the judiciary, as Lord Mansfield. She knocks upon the study door.

"Yes, Dido. Come," replies Lord Mansfield.

His nephew, Sir John Lindsay of the Royal Navy, is Dido's father. He captured a Spanish vessel and found a black woman, perhaps beautiful, perhaps a recaptured slave or kidnapped African princess, on board. A not-free, not-me woman. No one will say that Sir John Lindsay raped her, regardless of whether or not she was beautiful, or a slave. If we are to imagine it at all, we are to conjure a romance.

My darling, at last you've come. I thought you'd never find me. I've dreamt of you day and night, without ever knowing whether you were real. But I recognize you, my love, my savior! Deliver me from this captivity, and keep me with you always.

We are to imagine that something like *this* took place between a black woman from an undisclosed nation, likely non-English speaking, found on a captured Spanish ship, and a high-ranking naval officer with a chequered past. This brief encounter produced Dido Elizabeth Belle Lindsay, whose father, for reasons unknown, saw fit to both claim his biracial child *and* give her a name similar to her titled white cousin's. Then he left Dido in the care of the William Murrays and went back to running in the seas.

She was not left to follow the condition of her mother.

She enters her great-uncle's study.

No one seems to remember exactly what Dido's mother's condition was, how it might have improved, or worsened, after John Lindsay's touch. What her name was. Where she was when she gave birth. She seems to have simply disappeared from memory. Disappeared from care. Do you remember her, Dido? The years go back. It is 1772. After caring for the goats and chickens, a job she's reported to have enjoyed, she changes and knocks on her uncle's study. The room is consumed with papers about James Somerset, a former slave on British soil, threatened with a return to slavery by his former owner. Lord Mansfield settled Somerset's problem by granting him freedom, but let the question of slavery itself stand. Did you plug your ears, then, Dido? Or did you hear the talk? Did you cover your eyes, or did you read the papers? Did you clamp your mouth shut, or did you dare, just once, to speak on it? Your problem, Dido, is why it seems crucial to enclose the maximum area of your biography within a fixed boundary of silence.

The years go by.

"Naturally the presence of a black woman enjoying the close confidence of Mme de B. had to be explained," Ourika tells the doctor who's come to her convent to cure her of dying. "These explanations martyred me."

She realizes that she's African, and that fact becomes her illness. Only hers. Her hands seem to her monkey paws. "She exaggerates her ugliness," but her looks are not described by anyone in any terms. Where does her understanding of blackness equaling ugliness come from? Ourika sympathizes with the uprising in Haïti, yet feels shame for belonging to a race of murderous savages. She hates herself, not the fact of racism. *You're absolutely not our type. No one in France can identify with you.* It makes her sick.

Mme de B., speaking to her more blunt acquaintance, admits to being troubled, worried, about Ourika's marriage prospects, but is incapable of anything more. There's no Oroonoko in her future, no Equiano or any other possible equal. The fixed boundary of de Duras' literary imagination contains the maximum possibility for Ourika's happiness. Ourika becomes animal, a black angel of death, but she's not roaming in Melville's jungle, saving immoral white men from themselves. It's her own life that she must sacrifice. To save her neck during the French Revolution, however, Claire de Duras returned to her mother's native land, Martinique, to claim a sizeable inheritance. But for Ourika, in the end, it's the nunnery or nothingness.

Dido knocks on the study door, enters. It's 1781. The *Zong* case is on Lord Mansfield's table: an insurance suit for "lost" cargo during a storm: slaves preemptively thrown overboard though alive during a Middle Passage run gone bad. The slave ship's name is actually *Zorg*, Dutch for "care," but the British can't see that. Her great-uncle stands by the leaded window of his study, lost in thought. Young Lady Elizabeth will marry soon, leaving Kenwood, and arm-in-arm strolls with Dido, behind. And me, Dido thinks. What about me? What is to be my future?

"I didn't regret being black," Ourika says. "I was told I was an angel. . . . I didn't know then that these innocent studies would ripen into such bitter fruit." Mme de B. throws Ourika a ball. They do an African dance, the comba, comprised of stately steps, which require that she strike a pose signifying an emotion, grief, love, triumph, despair. A kind of Senegalese forebear to vogueing. *La verité: un jeu.* Out-of-the-kumbla: what is the pose for this feeling? Where on your body do you put your hand? Her white dance partner wears a mask of black crepe. Ourika strikes a pose, thinking nothing of it.

I was told I was an angel. Dido lets her hand wander over the stacks of writs and decrees, decisions and denials. *My father hasn't come for some time.* Her hand wanders over slavery's documentation as if divining, waiting for sensation, information, to rise up from ink and parchment and into her veins. *Care. Mother. Zorg. Zong. Care not. Something of me began here.* In the papers of William Murray is a letter of manumission for Dido, and, in his will, a bequeath to her of £500, and £100 a year for life. It will be at least ten years, when the Murrays are near death, nearly out of her care, before Dido strikes out into the world on her own, a good forty years before the abolition of slavery. She marries a Charles Davinier (French? Martinican or Haïtian *gens de couleur?*), who risks it, who is himself the risk, or simply loves her, either way. He's clearly not after her money; her purse is rather light. They have children. They manage to pass through time undetected, ignored, or simply accepted as people. Dido's line is somehow secreted away, into the mainstream. In the 1970s, her gravesite is razed for a redevelopment scheme. No roses, seen? But plenty of Violets.

Somewhere in the Continuum of the Imaginary, Princess Tam Tam swings in a cage, singing of Haïti. "If I truly possesses some superiority of mind," Ourika opines, "some hidden quality, then it would be appreciated when my color no longer isolated me, as it had until then, in the heart of society." Ourika sits by her window, reflecting. Outside it is day; she sees only fearsome night. Her smooth skin and bright eyes beam from the clear windowpane, but her vision is filled with monsters barely contained by the French government's *Code Noir*.

There will be guests *ce soir*, Dido muses. The horses nod in the stable, the chickens she's just fed burble and cluck in the yard of their house. She sits on a low stool in the cow pasture, drinking her rose congou tea and nibbling at oatcakes from a tray in her lap. Kenwood Estate lumbers solidly along the tamed green hillside at her back. Her cousin, ensconced in the still pressure of the sitting room, pokes needle and red thread through a taut hoop of muslin, dreamlessly waiting to be married. It will be dinner, then, she continues, alone in the kitchen. Then only after I'll be seen, all charm and sparkling wit, to entertain the nobles whose sensibilities were just thoroughly plied with fine foods. Only then will it be time for me. Then I'll come out and show off my accomplishments.

Ourika tells her doctor she would have preferred to labor on a plantation, for then she would have a hut to go to at the end of her day, a man of her own race to love her, children to kiss. "Why hadn't I been left to follow my own destiny?"

.

After another long evening, Dido returns to her room to conjure, as she often does, a world she's pieced together from the
bits that come to her from the guests. Hints and whispers,
oblique repartees, fearful pronouncements of slavery's descent on British soil. At daybreak, she sits singing by her window, *I am here. Where are you?* a glittering soprano, stringing vow-
els like jewels on clear thread, an invisible garland carried
through London's airs. *I am here.* Francis Barber, Samuel John-
son's black servant and heir, turns on his heel at the sound,
dictionary in hand. Each utterance of the line is a measure of
her maximum area, her unknown biography taking shape.
Where are you? Barbadian madame Rachel Pringle leaving her
brothel, on her way to secure publication for Mary Prince's
slave narrative, stops to inspect the sky. *I am here.* Elizabeth
Rosina "Bronze" Clements pauses from cleaning Royal Acad-
emy sculptor Joseph Nollekens' miserly kitchen. Dido calls.
To her mother's image and Ourika's spirit. Dido calls out into
the Continuum from the fixed boundary of her human life.
To all the other unexplained presences living in isolation, living in community, in and out of the kumbla, beyond her ken,
beyond Kenwood.

The four parts of the world stand nude and muscular, endeavoring to hold up a sphere that is the world. Asia, bald save for her long braid, pivots a bit, arms raised but not quite in contact with the sphere of the world. She looks over her shoulder, curiously preoccupied with Europe, who stands majestically, arms fully extended above her head, hair upswept in a zephyr of unseen air. Europe's right hand grasps at an arc of the sphere while the other swings free behind her back. Her eyes are fixed rapturously on the heavens, mouth slightly ajar. Next to Europe is America, her head crowned with feathers. Her torso twists in the direction of her head, rightward, her eyes are downcast, fixed on a land somewhere below Europe's feet, yet her arms stretch behind her, not reaching up to do the work of holding the sphere, but instead reaching back toward Africa's waist. Africa, unperturbed, stands in a pose similar to Europe's. Her arms are outstretched, with one hand grasping the world. Her jaw is set firm; she does not gaze rapturously at the heavens. Instead her eyes are intent, as if on the sparrow or the north star. Her right ankle is shackled to a broken chain resting free on the dais. The broken chain says that she's free, but America's large foot bears down upon it.

UNEXPLAINED

PRESENCE

We're invited to view history through a *Regency House Party* hosted by Britain's Channel 4. How exciting, to live a reality not our own, and on television, no less! Who might you be, set in the mid-1800s? What would you wear? Let's project ourselves into this myth, this romance. Foot in the back, tighten that corset, ladies! Show off your charms. Gents, stuff them trousers with sacks of barley and get ready to throw your wallet!

The music begins. We snake into the house on the back of an unseen dolly, through the doorway, past the pair of bronze Negro and Negress floor lamps flanking the doorway, each holding up candelabras of lit tapers. We file past the servants; we are the spectacle. We are aware of no other. The light upon our entry to the manor comes from nowhere, or is simply divine. As we are. King George III's son, the Prince Regent, "showed his nation how to party." That "Regency period introduced us to celebrity." And to notoriety, such as the unfortunate African width of then-current Queen Charlotte Sophia's nose, she the Prince Regent's mother, but this mention is outside the shrunken lightbox of our narrative. The music is a buoyant, nuptial romp; we size each other up, delighted.

.

Hosting this house party is Mr. Gorell Barnes, a young man plucked from a suitably affluent background in contemporary London, and thrust before us, ever so graciously, into the role of leading man. He's twenty-eight, and master of this house that generates £10,000 a year (equivalent to more than £300,000 today). Where his money comes from is about as unclear as is the source of Austen's Mr. Darcy.

"I'm excited about living in history," says Gorell Barnes. As if he doesn't already! And that's the point, we suppose, of our being here at this party. Barnes feels himself supremely suited for the Darcy-ish role. History has to be entered deliberately, as a diorama or a wax museum. It has to be acted upon, acted out. Danced. Or, once Responsibility points the finger, History must be trampled back to the depths where it belongs. Since the deck is stacked in his favor, Gorell Barnes has some not-so-stiff competition from his six male guests for the most marriageable young lady in the house. Among the men are a well-to-do officer in the Royal Navy, a bad boy militiaman, an "amateur scientist," and a seductive musician.

Mr. Gorell Barnes' counterpart in class acts is a true life Countess Griaznov, although the Countess' income is "undisclosed." We raise our eyebrows, curious. Does she actually have any? She has competition as well, from the six other young women guests, their bosoms trussed up, their matronly chaperones maneuvering to broker the deal of "their" girl to one of the men. Marry up, marry well! The women learn to be demure, what it means to be "accomplished," and confront the social pecking order structured according to parentage and purse.

The lineup: a nouveau riche heiress whose father "may well have made his money in trade with the Empire, plantation slavery or the industrializing North," a sassy, able-bodied (read *zaftig*) but low-worth redhead, and her blonde, thinner, and more amenable counterpart in poverty and titlelessness. At bottom is Miss Francesca Martin, a traveling companion to one of the chaperones, and completely ineligible for marriage to any of the male guests. While they all must wear unbearable layers of clothing, remain segregated from the men, and use lemon to freshen their armpits, it is Miss Martin who must, for the weekly body washing, bathe last, in the gray and tepid water left behind by the women ranked before her. The men play billiards, and smoke, ride horses, shoot, play at pugilism and cards. The women sit. The chaperones scheme and bicker. We watch them all take their roles far more seriously than their historical context. Of course, they're living it, their fake *then* in the Continuum of our very real *now*.

Then suddenly, a letter arrives:

Dearest Mrs. Rogers,

I hope you will forgive my boldness, but the presence of Miss Tanya Samuel at your delightful gathering is sure to be a welcome addition to your proceedings. Her beauty, confi-

dence, and honesty make her invigorating company. She remains, however, unattached.

The missive is not signed, nor is the writer revealed. History, then, makes a sudden appearance, in the guise of Miss
Tanya Samuel, a West Indian heiress. Not passing, nor Jewish,
but black. Lovely. And perhaps improbable, this at a time when
nearly all the blacks in the West Indies were slaves, all the West
Indians were white and some of them were . . .

"Stunning," says Captain Glover.

"Yes, she is, indeed."

"Everything is done for."

"I'm making no plans to be agreeable to this young lady."

Her purse trumps the Countess' and the industrial heiress',
as does her real life, in some respects, as a successful fashion de-
signer and the sister of a real celebrity, singer Seal. Miss Samuel's income is nearly £6,000 a year. Treat her like a lady, or
some such just reward for being so credentialed.

"She's been the toast of the capital."

"Then what's she want to come *here* for?"

"Miss Samuel's luggage is sent on ahead. A wealthy heiress,
and a beauty as well, she enters the house at the top of the
pecking order, a prize catch for any of the gentlemen." Our announcer's style is straight out of *Lifestyles of the Rich and Famous.*

The women of the house party haven't seen Miss Samuel
yet. But we see her now.

We see her before all the rest, before she enters History. She is black and comely. She scoffs at the idea that a Regency lady's behavior must conform to the expectations of the hostess.

"That depends, doesn't it? That *really* depends," she says, full mouth set, haughty, slight gap in her teeth, lovely. She knows her own worth.

Mr. Gorell Barnes, the alpha male, is also determined that Miss Samuel have the comforts her rank demands. But the chaperones have loudly, cattily decided not to be nice to her. He cajoles them into giving her a nice room.

"Well, it absolutely stinks that somebody can walk in and everybody has to sort of shuffle around like a bunch of ... crabs."

"Intelligent, beautiful, and wealthy," says Captain Glover of the Royal Navy. "Right up my street." As he speaks, hands belonging to an unseen body are busy tying up his neckwear.

The younger women complain about the lovebirds sent ahead with Miss Samuel's luggage. The Countess threatens to eat them. Mr. Gorell Barnes tries to make amends.

"After all," quips the announcer, "with her fortune and looks, she *could* make him the perfect wife."

She arrives in the rain, under an umbrella. Is she afraid? Servants strew rose petals at her feet as she approaches the house from her carriage in the mud. A young man carries her valise. The servants bow as she enters the main hall.

The white women are insanely jealous by the sight.

"Miss Samuel is competition for the other ladies in the house, even the Countess," the announcer intones.

"My first impression of the house? Very grand and very . . . very, very *strange*. Everything is done for you and you're literally waited on hand and foot, which is something that I could get used to." Miss Samuel speaks earnestly into the camera.

Has she stepped *into* history, then, or *through* it? Her visage, so smooth and controlled as the maids remove her hat, her coat, so gently, with such care. The maids, the manservant watching, they too hold their faces together in this first rush, first flush, the flush must somehow be concealed. The pinkening of emotion—embarrassment, outrage, shame—for in these moments they must perform as they would in history, in these moments performing complete servitude they must conceal this historical anomaly, this discrepancy, within their faces. In this moment now, Miss Samuel's expression is as entitled as her white servants' faces are unimpeachable.

How must this history feel? Trying it on, the romance of it, free, rich, black, and young in 1841? From where have you come? Who loves you? How did you get your money? From an African prince heading up the trade in the motherland? Were you manumitted by a benevolent white daddy? Were you a noble adoptee? We will never know, for no one bothered to write you a story. You were simply inserted here, a black caret flashing between paragraphs.

■

"I don't know how I'm going to be received by the other guests because I'm very, very privileged, just under the Countess." *Under*? We've been had, for only *we* know the truth about the Countess. She hasn't got a sou, or three guineas to rub together for luck. But the Countess' body is worth no less for her being broke. It is we who are worth less, surely, for being forced to keep such a secret. We are made less, along with Miss Samuel. The Countess isn't rich. Yet we defer to the master narrative, that the Countess *should* be rich. We could ask Miss Samuel, what is your body worth? Your love? Who here will show you? How will you conceal the shudder of walking through the doorway to the main sitting room, the doorway flanked with two inanimate objects in the form of Africans, standing barefoot, wearing turbans, lacquered, primitive, holding up lamps for you to see by?

"She doesn't need deportment lessons, that's for sure," says Captain Glover.

"No, she doesn't. Looks like she could teach us a thing or two."

Twinkling, waltzing piano and violin.

"It's a great opportunity to actually experience living the life of a black heiress. It's just nice to be able to enter into a house . . . of affluence, being on that level, and not being a maid, or a slave . . . for that matter."

Miss Samuel's maid shows her the makeup on the vanity, all

in tortoise cases and compacts, small, round lidded drums. The maid's hand lifts a lid. "Powder," she says, and her hand quivers, as if suddenly embarrassed. The powder is a translucent pinkish white as if from ground abalone shells. In an instant, we see the conflict between the powder and Miss Samuel's skin. It's clearly not the stuff of M.A.C. or Ebony Fashion Fair. The maid's hand hesitates, hovers. The real person under the maid's performance wants to cover the powder immediately, edit out its pink white with a quick drop of the lid, but the demand of the camera, and the unheard bark of the director, obviously forbids it. The maid's hand instinctively moves to replace the lid in the blink of an eye, then suddenly, as if on command, she yanks the lid back up. Miss Samuel *must* see the powder. *We* must see the powder.

"Because I'm sort of . . . if you like, new kid on the block, with all this luxury and privilege," Miss Tanya Samuel says, sitting at her vanity table, her face framed by an enormous rococo mirror glass, a white maid behind her, near invisible, coiling her lady's hair.

She doesn't look directly at us, or at herself, her face framed in the mirror glass. She cannot look directly on herself. No haughtiness; she is humbled by something we dare not name. The camera pulls back.

"I'm feeling a bit . . . *disadvantaged*, funnily enough, with all my advantages."

The room is sumptuous. Her vanity stands before Palladian

windows, a chaise lounge draped in finery, hand-painted fire-place plate, her gown swelling around her, a hand-woven rug under her feet.

"That's a bit daunting, really."

Miss Samuel is at the top of the procession to dinner, on the arm of Mr. Gorell Barnes, trailed by the Countess and some-one else.

"I hope you feel welcome," says Mr. Gorell Barnes. "Do you like your bedroom?"

Miss Samuel, taken aback, says something suitably demure to a remarkably untoward inquiry such as his. Gorell Barnes is barely gone when all the women surrounding Miss Samuel burst into laughter. But it's not all fun and games; something is at stake here. Winning. And bedding!

"You were *instantly* attracted to her," one of the chaperones accuses Captain Glover. "I'm concerned for your interest in my charge." She eyes Captain Glover hard. Something in him shrinks.

Mr. Gorell Barnes announces, "This is our Caribbean dinner evening in Miss Samuel's honor. We will be eating lots of . . . sweet . . . Caribbean . . . foods."

Crabmeat. Callaloo soup. Turtle soup.

The camera wanders over Miss Samuel's décolletage as she leans to spoon her soup, then frames only her breasts in close-up. The facets in the diamond-like baubles plunging into her cleavage lose their sharpness. We are that close. Do we want to touch? To smell, to sense . . . the romance? *Would you like to take a turn about the room?*

The camera leaves Miss Samuel's cleavage at last and pans down the table covered with confections. A smiling young black boy pulling a donkey. A windmill. Banana trees. Cane fields.

"Emphasis was placed on the decorative, and in a trend set by the Prince Regent's French Chef Antoine Caréme, large and elaborate sugar sculptures adorned the table as centerpieces," the announcer tells us.

"It's a controversial scene," explains Miss Hopkins, the industrial heiress whose father made his money with the Empire, either through slavery or the industrializing North.

"It's a sugar plantation, yes."

Miss Hopkins gives her bottom lip a flex, in either "hmmph" or "so what?" fashion.

"Although trade in slaves was abolished in 1807," the announcer cuts in, "many of Britain's great estates were built up from the income from slavery-produced sugar. Including *this* one. Now, with an abolitionist in the house—"

"*Who?*" cries the crowd. What makes a West Indian heiress candidate for abolitionism?

"—the guests must confront the truth behind their lavish lifestyle."

"Right. Hmmm."

"Of course slavery was wrong. But who were the first to discuss it, who were the first to abolish it but we English?" Mrs. Enright, a silver-haired chaperone, intones. In her "real" life, she is a decorated military officer.

Excited to step back into history, but not live it, the roles played by the guests at this *Regency House Party* fall away.

"I don't want to feel guilt for something I've never done or would never do," says Miss Hopkins.

"Right. Hmmm."

In Time but not of Time. In History but not of History. Everyone but Miss Tanya Samuel, it seems, exists outside the Continuum. They no longer want to play the roles of women seeking husbands in 1840s England, fully complicit in the moral and ethical slippages of their time. Miss Samuel rocks almost imperceptibly side to side, her mouth set, her brows raised in expression that might say "typical," that might say, "samo samo." They've instantly dropped their roles and have become contemporary. Or have they dropped their roles at all? They eat sumptuously. They dress well. They are heirs and heiresses of one type or another. Of lineage, social standing and social mores. They are not responsible. They don't ask where the money comes from. Captain Glover of the Royal

154

Navy might have been sent to intercept slave ships once the trade in (but not the use or forced reproduction of) slaves is abolished, but he doesn't seem to know his history. Their masks drop to reveal other masks.

Miss Samuel tells them how, once captured, Africans were dehumanized, made into slaves. Forgetting her role, she speaks in the past tense of the beatings, torture, and depravation known as the *seasoning* of slaves, as they eat Caribbean food prepared in her honor, at a table decorated with a plantation scene made out of sparkling sugar while slavery, meanwhile, currently disrupts the Cosmos. And yet, Gorell Barnes is the hero in all this. Is this not his house, his staff, his plan, all at his command? Was this dessert his idea? Miss Samuel is not indignant toward him. She does not ask him that. The roles then, are only partially played by the chosen civilians. Behind the scenes are other people, manipulating prejudice, perpetuating myth.

As she schools the party on the peculiar institution, Mr. Gorell Barnes stares at Miss Tanya Samuel. Is it love? Will it be allowed?

Then a man's voice: "Who said it was rude to talk politics over the table?"

"It *is* rude," replies one of the chaperones in a dull voice.

In and out of character.

"So, did you enjoy the sugar?" Captain Glover looks earnest. "Or do you prefer honey?"

"I do prefer honey, in fact. As Mr. Gorell Barnes knows." She and Gorell Barnes look at each other, then she looks around the table. Her chin rises defiantly. Her eyes point. The guests avert their gaze, looking to each other for support.

Gorell Barnes, the hero, puffs out his chest. Somewhat. A boycott is imposed, a mere twenty-four hours, in which sugar and tobacco will not be used. There is a great flapping of arms, snapping of jaws and flashing eyes. No sugar! No tobacco! Unheard of! Lucky for him he didn't include tea.

Later, in private, the young women are discussing the resistance to the boycott. They want to be given a choice. Mr. Gorell Barnes gives none. This is the last overture made in Miss Samuel's direction. She is clearly not a viable candidate for romance, not a rival for his affection, but a *cause* by which to further ennoble himself. By the next scene, Miss Tanya Samuel, Miss Tanya Ourika plays caretaker of *other* people's futures, scheming to bring the white women and men closer together, knowing full well that romance is not in the offing for herself. Talk of the boycott or of slavery is effectively quashed when Miss Victoria Hopkins, the industrial heiress, cuts in.

"As much as this is a really good debate, there are some things *far* more important."

They all giggle. A dandy is coming to town.

In a cutaway shot, a tall, thin black man in tight white breeches and long black shoes gambols, foot-light, down the east approach to the Estate. Flashes of scenes from an imagined history. Miss Hopkins reads aloud from the local *Gazette* that Mr. Austin Howard, a popular fellow in social circles, is in town. Why this excites her, or all the other women, what could come of it, remains unsaid. He appears as no one's guest, no one's possibility, and displays little recognized talent for anything but bulging breeches. He blends into the background of the house party scene just as mysteriously as he arrived.

"Without money or status," our back-to-the-future guide announces, "there were few opportunities for black people to enter society. Musical talent offered a rare way in."

"There's no other way to say it," confides Mrs. Enright to her camera-confessor. "He's black. Very *handsomely* black, with a very, very charming personality."

But black just the same.

Austin Howard never speaks to the camera, divulging his deepest secrets, inability to settle down, his need for honesty or a better bed. Perhaps he is more of a "someone" somewhere else, outside the frame. But Austin Howard is a dandy, a popular one, news of him creating a swoon–music here used euphemistically, with shots of his big feet. Like the rose petals tossed at Miss Samuel's feet, the young women fling themselves to the ground beneath Austin Howard's boots.

"What a welcome," he exclaims.

They rise, tittering, then scamper off.
"Such gaiety!" he cheeses.

Austin Howard conducts a quartet of blond school children, the scene reduced to a quick blur without comment (and whose children were these, being schooled by a free black dandy in the 1840s?), but doesn't seem to see Miss Tanya Samuel. They are never onscreen together. And besides, he's broke, and never utters a word after his arrival. He is poor and neuter. Miss Tanya Samuel is the richest chick in the house and desexed. None of the other men pretend, even just for the drama of it, to woo her, to be after her money. With a twinkling sweep of plantation sugar, Miss Tanya Samuel is transformed (transforms herself?) from intimidating, poised, and beautiful West Indian heiress, the richest of the women present, to magical, matchmaking Negro, holding up a bold light for others to see their futures by. As a nun might guide one's spirit toward eternal reward, before going to join the angels herself . . . Tanya Ourika Samuel is born.

"Oooh!" cries the crowd.
Such gaiety.

The Countess invites Gunter von Hagens to the house party.
"The Regency *was*, after all, the era that invented the autopsy."
Kentchurch.

"Plastinates."

The Countess asserts the body, her body, over all others. Alpha woman. She serves herself up, quite literally, as a dish, lays herself out, looking quite nude, but covered in food, on the dining room table. They eat from her body. We recall her secret is that she has no money, not a sou or three guineas to rub together for luck, but her titled body has worth above all others. And so it follows that she takes it upon herself to invite a German "doctor" to perform an autopsy in the house.

Discussion is wide-ranging, passionate. Dead bodies are permissible dinner topics. Rare beef is served. Von Hagens describes taking the body apart, bone by sinew by organ, and the process of plastinating them. There is no protest. Slavery cannot be discussed at dinner although it makes the dinner possible. But this talk has a sexual subtext. Somehow. Sweetmeats. They engage fully into the macabre, into the ethics and morality of this activity. But not the peculiar institution. They get close up. They get curious. They wonder at the identity of a plastinated female corpse. Much as they are repulsed, they want to know whose bodies these were. Where they came from. They want to touch.

"I feel compelled to look and look and look."

"He was looking at me like he wanted my body. Like he *really* wanted my body."

Apart from the partially fabricated eye of the corpse, it's all very, completely real.

The Countess looks triumphant. She's shaken things up on a libidinal level, which is what's important here. The atmosphere is positively corporeal. She's become the *Darling* of the house, and flaunting the moral convention of the time, she sleeps with Gorell Barnes and proclaims herself "winner." No enraged chaperone cries "Foul!" The ring, we suppose, is to come later.

Throughout this sequence, Miss Tanya Ourika Samuel, in her yellow dress, is scarce, and with each subsequent scene of a corpse, exposed skin, illicit romance, and sexual amorousness, she recedes further still into the background, taking with her the memory of dead Africans, the windmill powering the sugar mill, the smiling black boy, the banana trees and feathered turbans. The bronze Negro and Negress at the doorway hold their lamplights high behind her fading back.

The past is not past. This triple dimension of time, past, present, future, for me does not really exist. The past is only past in time; in reality, in our consciousness, the past is present, and that which we call future is nothing else than the dreamlike dimension of tomorrow experienced in the present.

THEO ANGELOPOULOS

CREDITS

FILMS

Darling. Dir. John Schlesinger. Embassy Pictures, 1965.

8 Femmes. Dir. François Ozon. Focus Features, 2002.

L'Eclisse. Dir. Michelangelo Antonioni. Times Film Corporation, 1962.

Le Samouraï. Dir. Jean Pierre Melville. Artists International, 1967.

Mansfield Park. Dir. Patricia Rozema. Miramax Films, 1999.

Sammy and Rosie Get Laid. Dir. Stephen Frears. Cinecom Pictures, 1987.

THEATRE

Compleat Female Stage Beauty. By Jeffrey Hatcher. Dir. Connie Crawford. Brown University. Stuart Theatre, Catherine Bryan Dill Center for the Performing Arts, Providence, RI. 11 March 2005.

SCULPTURES, OBJETS D'ART

Anonymous (various artifacts). *The Image of the Black in Western Art, Vol I: From the Pharaohs to the Fall of the Roman Empire*. Menil Foundation. New York: William Morrow and Co., 1976.

Furet, Andre. *Negress Clock Case*. 1785. Hillwood Museum and Gardens, Washington, DC.

Carpeaux, Jean-Baptiste. *The Four Parts of the World*. 1874. Jardins du Luxembourg, Paris. Personal Photographs of the author. 22 July 2001.

ENGRAVINGS, ILLUSTRATIONS, PAINTINGS

Anonymous. *Francis Williams*. 1740. Victoria and Albert Museum. *Black London: Life Before Emancipation*. By Gretchen Holbrook Gerzina. New Brunswick: Rutgers University Press, 1995. Plate 6.

Grimm, S. H. "Heyday! is this my Daughter Anne." 1771. *Drolleries*. Print Collection, Lewis Walpole Library, Yale University. *Black London: Life Before Emancipation*. By Gretchen Holbrook Gerzina. New Brunswick: Rutgers University Press, 1995. Plate 1.

Hogarth, William. *Four Times of Day—Noon*. 1738. *Hogarth's Blacks: Images of Blacks in Eighteenth Century Art*. By David Dabydeen. Atlanta: University of Georgia Press, 1987. 61.

Ramsay, Allan. *Charlotte Sophia of Mecklenburg-Strelitz*. 1762. National Portrait Gallery, London. *Black Beauty: A History and a Celebration*. By Ben Arogundade. New York: Thunder's Mouth Press, 2001. 18.

Zoffany, Johann. *Dido and Lady Elizabeth Finch Hatton*. 1779. Earl of Mansfield. London. *Black London: Life Before Emancipation*. By Gretchen Holbrook Gerzina. New Brunswick: Rutgers University Press, 1995. Cover.

TELEVISION

Regency House Party. Dir. Tim Carter. Narr. Richard E. Grant. DVD. PBS Home Video, 2004.

TEXTS

Angelopoulous, Theo. Interview. *The Weeping Meadow*. DVD. New Yorker Films, 2003.

Bachelard, Gaston. "Intimate Immensity." *The Poetics of Space*. Trans. Maria Jolas. Boston: Beacon Press, 1969.

Chirico, Giorgio de. *Hebdomeros: A Novel*. Boston: Exact Change, 2004.

DuPlessis, Rachel Blau. "For the Etruscans." *The Pink Guitar: Writing as Feminist Practice*. New York: Routledge, 1990.

Duras, Claire de. *Ourika: An English Translation*. Trans. John Fowles. New York: The Modern Language Association, 1994.

Glissant, Eduoard. "The Open Boat." *Poetics of Relation*. Trans. Betsy Wing. Ann Arbor: The University of Michigan Press, 1997.

Minh-ha, Trinh T. "Cotton and Iron." *When the Moon Waxes Red: Representation, Gender and Cultural Politics*. New York: Routledge, 1991.

Morrison, Toni. "Disturbing Nurses and the Kindness of Sharks." *Playing in the Dark: Whiteness and the Literary Imagination*. Cambridge: Harvard University Press, 1992.

Woolf, Virginia. *Orlando*. London: The Hogarth Press, 1928

Zola, Emile. "Une nouvelle maniere en peinture, Eduoard Manet" (originally published in *Revue du XIXe Siecle 4*, no. 10, 1 January 1867, 58–59). *The Image of the Black in Western Art, Volume IV: From the American Revolution to World War I; Part 2: Black Models and White Myths*. Ed. Hugh Honour. Menil Foundation, Inc. Cambridge: Harvard University Press, 1989. 159.

REVIEWS

Rosenbaum, Jonathan. Rev. of *Le Samouraï*, dir. Jean-Pierre Melville. *The Chicago Reader on Film*. www.chicagoreader.com/film/filling-in-the-blanks-3.

Afterw

word

You have just finished reading this book. It has treated you as a reader, a spectator, and a traveler. Each chapter—its prose, its structure, its sensory abundance—mimics or recreates a film scene, a painting, a stage set, adding inflections, ambiguities, and questions. Tisa Bryant is a literary and film auteur, an auteur of performance on the page, stage, screen, or canvas. She moves from the realm of the senses to the realm of speculation, from rich analysis to richly descriptive narrative.

As Bryant has told us, the presence of black figures (objects and characters) in Eurocentric art goes "unexplained" because its meanings are so taken for granted. Exotic emotional and sexual transgressions, alluring violence, racial and gender sleights of hand that stand in for real meaning. The task she has so daringly given herself is to reframe and rewrite; to see, hear, feel, and think past these confines.

Bryant uses her opening chapter (or "Scene") to recreate the opening of John Schlesinger's Darling, the iconic 1965 film that starred the iconic Julie Christie as the iconic supermodel Diana Scott, blonde and smiling "hair swinging carefree over London's soft-focus bustle." . . . Ah yes, we remember it well, don't we? But do we also remember that Darling opens with "a white frame, a billboard of emaciated children from foodless nations, figured in charcoal and stippled inks, glimpsed as if through fast blinking eyes"? How did we—I, you, they, how in fact did I—manage to distance or forget this other guiding image at the film's opening? Schlesinger does it for us, Bryant observes, with the image of a white workman papering these bodies over with the face of the "Ideal Woman." But we will not be able to do it ourselves after reading Bryant. Her language binds these two disparate images together as the paragraph ends. Look at Darling/Diana again. Look at "Those lips. Those eyes. Those dark and morbid bones beneath the teeth." Bryant has absorbed and redirected our gaze. Now the black children and the white women are joined, filmic totems and taboos, playing their part on the white expanse—the patriarchal billboard—of British culture.

Now turn to the book's last essay or "Scene Selection." The year is 2004, and we have been invited to *Regency House Party*, a TV series hosted by Britain's Channel 4 where au courant reality meets historical reenactment. "The music begins," Bryant writes in voice-over mode. "We snake into the house on the back of an unseen dolly, through the doorway, past the pair of bronze Negro and Negress floor lamps flanking the doorway, each holding up candelabras of lit tapers." These lamps will cast their flickering light on all plot twists to come: the sexual spats, the social jousts; the thrust and parry of race and gender. These reality show characters are living "their fake *then* in the Continuum of our very real *now*." How then do we situate ourselves, Bryant asks as she narrates, frames, and interprets. She makes herself a cultural anthropologist, she becomes the narrator as participant-observer. She constructs a kind of ethnography for *Regency House Party* with its mixed genres, mixed time frames, and mixed motives.

She does this with each film she chooses, adjusting her tone, her style to its particular demands. She probes the uses of each image the possibilities of each metaphor however brief its appearance. In the closing sequence of *Regency House Party*, the ascent of a scheming white countess ensures the descent of a Black West Indian heiress. Bryant describes the heiress as receding further and further into the background, taking with her the "unexplained presence" of British race crimes: "the memory of dead Africans, the windmill powering the sugar mill, the smiling black boy, the banana trees and feathered turbans. The bronze Negro and Negress at the doorway hold their lamplights high behind her fading back."

Bryant has made these figures her spirit guides. And by using them as symbols that gesture to more rather than fewer meanings, she has become our—the Readers'—spirit guide. In these the oh-so-familiar racialized figures (manipulative black maid, grieving black mother, sultry black nightclub temptress), she finds overlooked intentions and unanswered questions.

A suave and jaded Italian woman dons blackface makeup (Antonioni's *L'eclisse*); a virile young aristocrat slices at a Moor's head that swings from the rafters of his family castle (Woolf's *Orlando*); a black queer man is cast as the white queer man who was the last of his sex to play a woman on the London stage (Jeffrey Hatcher's *Compleat Female Stage Beauty*).

Bryant's language is probing yet sumptuous; it brings us so close to an engraving or art object that we feel we're merging with it. The structure of the book moves like a montage or film essay, linking retellings of film and literary narratives with shorter ekphrastic pieces and epigraphs, interstitial moments that point the way back and forward. In one of my favorite moments, she has us read a museum description of a bust-size eighteenth-century Negress clock case. Then, three pages later, she uses it to create her own short, fantastical film: An English queen, rumored to have black ancestors is being painted; magically (by means of the clock case and a clever painter) we witness her hair straighten, her nostrils narrow, and her skin pinken.

I've called Bryant an auteur, a cultural anthropologist, and a spirit guide. I'll end by calling her a virtuosic critic-artist. *Unexplained Presence* was ahead of its time in 2007 when it was first published. Happily, for us it still is. Turn back to that first page. Turn back to any page you wish. Start reading again.

MARGO JEFFERSON

2023